Joint Staff Study: ICEBERG Operation

Contents

Joint Staff Study: ICEBERG Operation

Headquarters United States Pacific Fleet And Pacific Ocean Areas

Nimble Books LLC: The AI Lab for Book-Lovers

Fred Zimmerman, Editor

Humans and AI making books richer, more diverse, and more surprising

Publishing Information

- (c) 2024 Nimble Books LLC
- ISBN: 978-1-60888-337-0

Nimble Books LLC ~ NimbleBooks.com

Bibliographic Key Phrases

ICEBERG Operation; Joint Staff Study; U.S. Pacific Fleet; Pacific Ocean Areas; Okinawa; Iwo Jima; Nansei Shoto; Ryukyu Islands; Military Government; Care of Civilians; Logistic Measures; Force Requirements; Airfield Development; Naval Facilities; Phase I; Phase II; Phase III; MIYAKO JIMA; KIKAI SHIMA; OKINO DAITO JIMA; KUME SHIMA; Troop List; Air Operations; Naval Operations; Submarine Operations; Target Dates; Logistics; Evacuation;

Publisher's Note

The ongoing debates about the role of the military in modern society demand a nuanced understanding of historical precedent. This document, a Top Secret Joint Staff Study from the U.S. Pacific Fleet and Pacific Ocean Areas, provides a fascinating glimpse into the operational planning behind the pivotal battle for Okinawa during World War II. It delves into the strategy and tactics employed to seize and develop bases in the Nansei Shoto, examining the complex interplay between military, political, and logistical considerations in the Pacific Theater.

The study goes beyond a mere chronological account of the campaign, offering valuable insight into the complexities of warfighting. It reveals critical details about Japanese defensive capabilities, military force requirements, and the challenges of securing and sustaining operations in a remote and hostile environment. Notably, the document features detailed annexes providing troop lists, logistical blueprints, and the conceptualization of naval and air operations, offering a unique opportunity to analyze the operational thinking and resource allocation during a pivotal moment in World War II.

Whether you are a military historian, a policymaker grappling with the modern implications of force projection, or simply someone intrigued by the intricacies of wartime operations, this document provides a compelling narrative and valuable insights. It reveals the strategic and logistical challenges of achieving victory in a major conflict, offering a stark reminder of the immense costs and complexities of war. A must-read for anyone seeking to understand the evolution of warfare and its enduring influence on the world today.

This annotated edition illustrates the capabilities of the AI Lab for Book-Lovers to add context and ease-of-use to manuscripts. It includes publishing information; abstracts; viewpoints; learning aids; and references.

Abstracts

TLDR (three words)

Seize Okinawa, 1945

ELI5

This is a secret plan from World War II for how the United States would capture the island of Okinawa from Japan. It's like a big game of strategy, with soldiers, ships, and airplanes all working together to win. The plan explains who will do what, where they will go, and what supplies they will need.

Scientific-Style Abstract

This document, declassified in 1972, details the Joint Staff Study, "ICEBERG," outlining the U.S. Pacific Fleet and Pacific Ocean Areas' plan for the capture and occupation of Okinawa in 1945. It provides a detailed analysis of the Japanese defenses, projected enemy capabilities, and the necessary troop and naval deployment for three distinct operational phases. The plan addresses logistic requirements for troop transport, supply chains, and base development, including airfields, harbors, and medical facilities. Notably, "ICEBERG" addresses civilian care and the establishment of military government in the conquered territories. This document offers a valuable insight into the strategic planning and logistical complexities of a major amphibious operation during World War II.

Five Key Takeaways

Here are five key takeaways from the "ICEBERG" document:

1. **Okinawa was a crucial strategic objective:** The document emphasizes Okinawa's strategic importance for the U.S. in their effort to defeat Japan. Controlling the island would allow the U.S. to:
   - Launch air and naval attacks on the Japanese mainland.
   - Sever Japanese communication lines.
   - Establish a secure base for future operations in the East China Sea.
   - Maintain pressure on Japan and deny them access to crucial resources.
2. **The operation was divided into three phases:** The plan was designed in three phases, each focusing on specific objectives:
   - **Phase I:** Secure the southern portion of Okinawa, including satellite islands, and develop essential base facilities.
   - **Phase II:** Capture the remainder of Okinawa and the island of I-Ie Shima, with emphasis on securing and developing airfields.
   - **Phase III:** Capture and develop additional positions in the Ryukyu Islands (Miyako and Kikai), further extending air and naval operations against Japan.

3. **Logistical complexities were paramount:** The document meticulously outlines the logistical challenges and solutions, including:
   - Troop transport and staging.
   - Supply chain management for ammunition, fuel, food, and medical supplies.
   - Building and maintaining airfields and harbors.
   - Ensuring adequate medical care for both soldiers and civilians.
4. **The operation anticipated fierce Japanese resistance:** The plan acknowledges the Japanese determination to defend their territory and anticipates heavy fighting. It includes strategies for:
   - Destroying Japanese air defenses and preventing reinforcements.
   - Utilizing overwhelming naval fire support.
   - Employing amphibious maneuvers to exploit weaknesses in Japanese defenses.
5. **Civilian care and military government were factored in:** Despite the military focus, the document acknowledges the humanitarian concerns of a large civilian population:
   - The plan includes measures for providing food, water, shelter, and medical care to civilians.
   - It outlines the establishment of military government to manage conquered territory, ensuring law and order while potentially using civilian labor for reconstruction efforts.

Learning Aids

Mnemonic (acronym)

K.I.K.A. - **K**ume, **I**wo Jima, **K**ikai, **A**mami

Mnemonic (speakable)

Okinawa *is where we land* - **IE Shima** *is next in line* - **Miyako** *is for long-range bombers* - **Kikai** *is for the fighter planes*

Mnemonic (singable)

To the tune of "My Bonnie"

Okinawa is our first stop IE Shima we will take next Miyako for long-range bombers Kikai's for fighter jets

Okinawa is our first stop IE Shima we will take next Miyako for long-range bombers Kikai's for fighter jets

We'll be ready by March 1st When we conquer the Nansei Shoto We'll be ready by March 1st When we conquer the Nansei Shoto

Innovations

Here are three short, innovative learning aids to help a reader absorb the content of the book about "ICEBERG," presented entirely as text:

1. Timeline of the Operation:

Key Dates:

- **D-Day:** March 1, 1945 - Initial landing on Okinawa (Phase I).
- **W-Day:** March 31, 1945 - Initial landing on I-Ie Shima (Phase II).
- **A-Day:** May 10, 1945 - Initial landing on Miyako (Phase III).
- **F-Day:** June 10, 1945 - Initial landing on Kikai (Phase III).

Key Events:

- **Phase I:** Capture of Southern Okinawa and base development: The focus was on securing the southern half of Okinawa, including satellite islands, to establish a beachhead and build essential bases.
- **Phase II:** Capture of I-Ie Shima and expansion of air bases: The plan included seizing the strategically important I-Ie Shima to construct more airfields, expanding air power in the region.
- **Phase III:** Capture of Miyako and Kikai, extending air and naval operations: The operation aimed to secure Miyako as a base for long-range bombers and Kikai for fighter operations, furthering the blockade of Japan.

2. Okinawa: A Strategic Puzzle:

Puzzle Pieces:

- **Southern Okinawa:** This area was targeted for initial capture due to its extensive flat land suitable for harbor and airfield development, but was heavily defended by the Japanese.
- **Northern Okinawa:** This mountainous area was expected to be defended lightly, offering a potential path for flanking maneuvers and securing the entire island.
- **I-Ie Shima:** This small island, close to Okinawa, offered a valuable location for constructing additional air bases to expand American air power.
- **Miyako Island:** This larger island, further south, was a crucial objective to establish a base for long-range bombers to directly attack the Japanese mainland.
- **Kikai Island:** This island, positioned closer to the Japanese mainland, was intended to be a fighter base, providing air cover for operations and protection for the other islands.

Challenge:

The reader must mentally assemble these puzzle pieces, recognizing the logical progression of the operation, the importance of each objective, and the overall strategic goal.

3. Logistic Bingo:

Bingo Card:

Columns:

- **Column 1:** AvGas, LST, Water Purification Units
- **Column 2:** Military Government, Medical Evacuation, Supply Chain Management
- **Column 3:** Tank Farm, Aircraft Spares, Construction Equipment
- **Column 4:** Pontoon Piers, Harbor Defense, Ammunition Stockpiles
- **Column 5:** Food Supplies, Drummed Fuel, Prisoner of War Camps

Challenge:

As you read the book, mark off any element from the Bingo card when it is discussed in the document. The goal is to achieve Bingo by marking five squares in a row, horizontally, vertically, or diagonally.

Learning Outcome:

This exercise encourages active reading and helps readers identify and recall the critical logistical components of the "ICEBERG" operation.

References

Glossary

This glossary defines terms used in the Joint Staff Study, ICEBERG Operation, and other historical documents from this time period, that a lay reader might not understand. It is not meant to be an exhaustive list of terms.

A-Day: The first day of the amphibious invasion of MIYAKO JIMA in Operation ICEBERG. The date of A-Day is a moving target, dependent on the availability of forces. The authors of the document estimate A-Day as L+90 (90 days after the initial landing on OKINAWA).

AAFPOA: "Army Air Forces, Pacific Ocean Areas". This is a military command responsible for planning and conducting air operations in the Pacific. This command was subordinate to the Commander-in-Chief, Pacific Ocean Areas (CinCPac).

Advanced Base: A military base used for staging operations forward of the main base of operations. It is frequently located closer to an enemy's territory and can be supplied from the main base of operations, often by sea or air.

AH: Amphibious Hospital Ship. These specialized ships provided medical care and evacuation for injured military personnel.

AK: "Attack Cargo" Ship. This was a class of cargo ships used to transport goods and supplies. They were usually smaller than the larger troop transports, and they typically had a lower capacity for carrying passengers.

Air warning: A warning of enemy air activity, often relayed by radar, that an air defense unit can use to prepare to intercept enemy aircraft.

Airborne: Used to describe troops or equipment transported by air and deployed in combat by parachute, glider, or fixed-wing aircraft.

Amphibious: Used to describe operations involving a landing from the sea onto the shore. Amphibious operations typically involve the use of landing craft (LCVP, LCM, LCT, LST) and specialized ships that can transport troops and equipment.

Anti-aircraft (AA): A type of weaponry that is designed to engage enemy aircraft, primarily used to defend ground troops and assets from air attack.

Anti-submarine (ASW): A type of warfare focused on detecting and destroying enemy submarines. This warfare typically involves the use of sonar, depth charges, and specialized ships.

AP: "Attack Transport" Ship. This was a class of ships designed to transport troops and cargo in amphibious operations.

APH: "Attack Transport (Hospital)" Ship. This class of ship was modified to provide medical care and evacuation for injured personnel.

Area reserve: A reserve force that is not committed to a specific operation but is held ready to deploy to any location as needed.

Artillery: Heavy weapons that are designed to launch explosive projectiles (shells) at a target, typically at a long distance.

Avgas: "Aviation Gasoline". This is a type of gasoline specifically blended for use in aircraft.

Avlube: "Aviation Lubricating Oil". This is a special type of oil designed for use in aircraft engines.

B-24: "Liberator" four-engine heavy bomber.

B-25: "Mitchell" medium bomber.

Base Supported: A unit that is supported by resources at a base, rather than by ships.

Battleships: Large warships that were designed for long-range bombardment. Battleships were heavily armored and equipped with large-caliber guns.

Bn: "Battalion". A battalion is a military unit consisting of between 300 and 1,000 personnel that is usually composed of several companies.

Bonins: A chain of islands known as the Bonin Islands, located to the south of Japan and north of the Mariana Islands.

Bulk: Used to describe items that are shipped in large, un-packaged quantities, such as oil or grain.

CA: "Cruiser". A medium-sized warship that is designed for a combination of combat roles, including surface warfare, anti-aircraft warfare, and escort missions.

Cargo Capy: "Cargo Capacity". A measure of how much cargo a ship can carry.

Caroliens: A group of islands known as the Caroline Islands, located in the western Pacific Ocean, south of the Mariana Islands and north of New Guinea.

CB: "Battleship (Cruiser)"

CentPac: "Central Pacific Area". This is the command responsible for planning and conducting operations in the Central Pacific.

CinC: "Commander-in-Chief". The highest ranking military commander in a specific area.

CinCPOA: "Commander-in-Chief, Pacific Ocean Areas"

CinCSWPA: "Commander-in-Chief, Southwest Pacific Area"

Cl: "Cruiser (Light)"

CL(AA): "Cruiser (Light, Anti-Aircraft)"

Combatant: Used to describe military units or ships that are involved in combat.

Combat air patrol: A mission flown by fighter aircraft to provide air defense over friendly forces.

Combat troops: Troops that are designated for fighting in combat operations, such as those involved in landings.

ComGen: "Commanding General". The highest ranking military commander in an army or corps.

ComGenPOA: "Commanding General, Pacific Ocean Areas"

ComGenFMFPac: "Commanding General, Fleet Marine Force, Pacific". The commander of the Marines in the Pacific.

ComGenAirF.FPac: "Commanding General, Fleet Marine Air Force, Pacific". The commander of the Marines' air component in the Pacific.

ComGenAAFPPOA: "Commanding General, Army Air Forces, Pacific Ocean Areas". The commander of the Army's air component in the Pacific.

ComFwdAreaCentPac: "Commander Forward Area, Central Pacific"

CominCh: "Commander-in-Chief, United States Navy"

CominPac: "Commander-in-Chief, Pacific Fleet"

ComPhibsPac: "Commander Amphibious Forces, Pacific Fleet"

ComServPac: "Commander Service Force, Pacific Fleet"

ComSoPac: "Commander, South Pacific Area"

ComSthFleet: "Commander 5th Fleet"

Com5thPhibFor: "Commander 5th Fleet Amphibious Forces"

Com7thFlt: "Commander 7th Fleet"

ComMarGilsArea: "Commander, Marianas Islands Area"

Construction material: Material needed to build roads, bridges, airfields, and other structures,

Convoy: A group of ships, often protected by warships, that are traveling together for mutual protection from attack.

Corps: A large military unit composed of several divisions.

CVE: "Escort Carrier"

CV: "Aircraft Carrier"

CVL: "Aircraft Carrier (Light)"

D-Day: The day of the initial amphibious landing on OKINAWA.

DE: "Destroyer Escort". Smaller warships, less heavily armed than destroyers, that were primarily used for escorting other ships and for anti-submarine warfare.

DETACIEENT: A military detachment sent to a specific location to carry out a mission.

Dispensary: A medical facility where patients can receive outpatient care.

Distribution List: A list of individuals and offices that are to receive copies of a document.

Division: A large military unit, usually composed of 10,000 to 15,000 personnel, that can include infantry, armor, artillery, and support units.

DM: "Landing Craft, Mechanized".

DUK: "Landing Craft, Vehicle".

East Indies: A region in Southeast Asia that includes the islands of Indonesia, Malaysia, Singapore, and the Philippines.

East China Sea: A sea located to the east of China and south of Korea.

Echelon: A level in a military organization, or a group of units that are deployed at the same time. For example, a division could be deployed in two echelons: the first echelon would land on the first day of the operation, and the second echelon would follow later.

Enemy: A hostile force, in this case the Imperial Japanese military.

Engineer Combat Bn: "Engineer Combat Battalion"

Engineer Gp: "Engineer Group"

Engr Avn Regt: "Engineer Aviation Regiment".

Engr Top Bn: "Engineer Topographic Battalion"

ENIWETOK: An atoll in the Marshall Islands in the Central Pacific.

ESFIRITU SANTO: An island in the Republic of Vanuatu.

Evacuation: The process of moving injured or sick personnel out of a combat zone, often by air or sea.

Expeditionary: Used to describe a military force that is deployed to a distant location to conduct a mission.

Expeditionary Force: The force of troops and ships that will conduct Operation ICEBERG.

Expeditionary Troops: The troops that are part of the Expeditionary Force.

Far Eastern Air Force (FEAF): This command was responsible for planning and conducting air operations against the Japanese in Southeast Asia and China.

Fathom: A unit of depth measurement that is equal to six feet (1.8 meters).

Fleet: A large group of warships, often under a single commander.

Fleet Marine Force (FMF): The U.S. Marines, who are deployed in support of the Navy.

Fleet Supported: A unit that is supported by ships.

Fleet Moorings: Mooring buoys, chains, or other equipment used to secure ships to the seafloor in an anchorage.

Floating repair facilities: Ships or barges that are equipped to perform repairs on other ships.

Floating reserve: A reserve force that is held in ships, rather than on land, ready to deploy as needed.

Form Approved: A designation that indicates that a document has been approved by a government agency.

Formosa: A large island located off the coast of China, previously under Japanese control, known today as Taiwan.

Fortress group: A military unit that is specifically designed to defend a fortification, such as a fort or a city.

FPO: "Fleet Post Office".

FP.O: "Field Post Office". A mobile post office that follows military units, delivering mail to the troops.

Forces Required: The number of troops and equipment that are estimated to be needed for an operation.

Forward Area: A region located closer to an enemy's territory, often near the front lines of a battle.

Formosa Strait: The body of water that separates Taiwan from mainland China.

Garrison: A military unit that is stationed at a base to defend it and provide security for the area.

Garrison Forces: Troops that will be stationed in Okinawa after the island is captured.

G-2: "Intelligence". A military unit responsible for collecting and analyzing intelligence about the enemy.

G-4: "Logistics". A military unit responsible for planning and supplying troops.

G-6: "Signal". A military unit responsible for communication.

G-8: "Personnel". A military unit responsible for the administration of personnel.

G-10: "Medical". A military unit responsible for providing medical care.

G-14: "Dental". A military unit responsible for providing dental care.

G-18: "Veterinary". A military unit responsible for providing veterinary care.

GTenAAFPOA: "General, Tenth Army Air Forces, Pacific Ocean Areas". The commander of the Army's air component in the Pacific.

GUAM: A large island in the Mariana Islands.

Guadalcanal: A large island in the Solomon Islands.

Gun: A type of weapon that fires projectiles.

Guns: In this document, usually refers to large artillery pieces, particularly those used for anti-aircraft or coastal defense.

Group: A military unit that is composed of several squadrons.

GROPAC: "Group, Reconnaissance, Pacific". A group of naval units that are responsible for providing reconnaissance and surveillance.

GVULF: "Group, Marine Fighter"

HECP: "Harbor Entrance Control Post".

HH: "Hospital Ship"

How: "Howitzer". A type of artillery that is designed to fire shells at a high trajectory, making it effective for reaching targets behind cover.

hvGas: "High-octane Aviation Gasoline"

I-Day: The day when Phase I of Operation ICEBERG is to be completed.

IE SHIMA: An island located off the northwestern coast of Okinawa.

Independent Mixed Brigade: A military unit that is not part of a division but is composed of infantry, artillery, and other units,

Infantry: Ground troops that are armed with small arms and are primarily used to conduct close combat operations.

Interdict: To stop or hinder the movement of enemy forces or supplies.

Interdiction: The process of stopping or hindering the movement of enemy forces or supplies, typically accomplished by air attacks or submarine patrols.

Internment: The process of confining individuals to a designated location.

Interned: Describes an individual or group of individuals who are confined to a designated location, such as a camp.

Internment camp: A facility designed to confine individuals, typically prisoners of war or civilians who are considered a threat to security.

IWO JIMA: A volcanic island located to the south of Japan.

JCS: "Joint Chiefs of Staff". The highest ranking military commanders from each branch of the United States military.

JFSC: "Joint Forces Staff College"

Junk Bay: A large bay on the eastern side of MIYAKO JIMA.

JASCO: "Joint Army-Navy Communications Office"

K-Day: The first day of the amphibious invasion of KIKAI in Operation ICEBERG. The date of K-Day is a moving target, dependent on the availability of forces. The authors of the document estimate K-Day as L+120 (120 days after the initial landing on OKINAWA).

KIKAI: An island located off the coast of Japan.

KOREA: A peninsula in East Asia.

KUMIVI SHIMA: An island located off the northwestern coast of Okinawa.

KYUSHU: One of the main islands of Japan.

L-Day: The day of the initial amphibious landing on OKINAWA. This is also known as D-Day.

LCVP: "Landing Craft, Vehicle, Personnel". These small boats were primarily used to transport troops from ships to shore.

LCM: "Landing Craft, Mechanized". These larger boats were used to transport troops and vehicles from ships to shore.

LCT: "Landing Craft, Tank". These large boats were designed to transport tanks and other heavy equipment.

LCI: "Landing Craft, Infantry"

LCI(G): "Landing Craft, Infantry (Gun)"

LCI(L): "Landing Craft, Infantry (Large)"

LCI(M): "Landing Craft, Infantry (Medium)"

LSM: "Landing Ship, Medium". These ships were designed to carry a greater cargo and troop capacity than landing craft, and they were capable of beach landings.

LST: "Landing Ship, Tank". These large ships were designed to transport tanks and other heavy equipment. They were able to land on beaches.

LSV: "Landing Ship, Vehicle". A ship designed to carry vehicles and cargo.

LSD: "Landing Ship, Dock". A ship that served as a floating dock for landing craft.

Lube: "Lubricating Oil". A type of oil used to reduce friction between moving parts.

LUZON: The largest island in the Philippines.

LVT: "Landing Vehicle, Tracked". These amphibious vehicles were used to transport troops and equipment from ships to shore.

Lvn: "Aviation fuel"

Mainland: Used to refer to the main part of a country or continent, as opposed to islands. For example, the authors of this document refer to the "mainland of ASIA", meaning mainland Asia.

Maintenance supplies: Supplies, such as spare parts, tools, and equipment, that are needed to keep military units operational.

MARIANAS: A group of islands located in the western Pacific Ocean.

Marine: A member of the United States Marine Corps.

MarDiv: "Marine Division"

Mar.iv: "Marine Division"

Marine Fighter: A fighter aircraft flown by Marines.

Marine Torpedo Bomber: A torpedo bomber aircraft flown by Marines.

Marine Night Fighter: A fighter aircraft flown by Marines that is specialized for combat at night.

Measurement ton: A unit of weight that is equal to 40 cubic feet (1.1 cubic meters).

Military government: A system of government that is imposed by a military force over a conquered or occupied territory.

Military yen: A special currency that was issued by the U.S. military during World War II to be used in occupied territories.

Minesweeping: The process of clearing a body of water of mines.

Minesweeping Group: A group of ships that are designed to conduct minesweeping operations.

Mission: A specific task that is assigned to a military unit.

Mogas: "Motor Gasoline". A type of gasoline used in vehicles and equipment.

Mortlock: The Mortlock Islands are a group of islands located east of the island of Chuuk in the Caroline Islands.

MIYAKO: An island located off the coast of Japan.

MIYAKO JIMA: An island located off the coast of Japan.

MIYAKO HETTO: "MIYAKO Islands"

MO: "Military Order"

Motobu Peninsula: A peninsula located on the northern end of Okinawa.

N-1: "Camp (Administration)". A military unit responsible for the administration of a camp.

N-2: "Camp (Housing)". A military unit responsible for providing housing in a camp.

N-4: "Camp (Service)". A military unit responsible for providing services in a camp.

N-5: "Camp (Buildings)". A military unit responsible for providing and maintaining buildings in a camp.

N-6: "Camp (Food Service)". A military unit responsible for food service in a camp.

N-7: "Camp (Administration)". A military unit responsible for the administration of a camp.

N-8: "Camp (Buildings)". A military unit responsible for providing and maintaining buildings in a camp.

N-9: "Camp (Recreation)". A military unit responsible for providing recreational facilities in a camp.

N-10: "Camp (Education)". A military unit responsible for providing educational facilities in a camp.

N-12: "Camp (Laundry)". A military unit responsible for providing laundry facilities in a camp.

NAHA: The largest city on the island of OKINAWA.

NAITSEI SHOTO: "Inner Islands". The main islands of Japan, as opposed to the outer islands and territories.

NANSEI SHOTO: "Southern Islands". A chain of islands located to the south of Japan.

NATS: "Naval Air Transport Service"

Naval Air Transport Service (NATS): A service responsible for air transport of troops, equipment, and supplies.

Naval Base: A base of operations for naval forces.

Naval Combatant: A warship.

Naval Personnel: Members of the Navy.

Naval Supply Depots: Warehouses where the Navy stores supplies.

Net: A type of barrier that is used to prevent enemy submarines or ships from entering an area.

Night Fighter: A fighter aircraft that is specialized for combat at night.

North China: The northern part of China, particularly the area north of the Yellow River.

Northern Luzon: The northern part of Luzon, the largest island in the Philippines.

OMB: "Office of Management and Budget". The part of the U.S. Government responsible for overseeing the budget.

Oiler: A ship that carries oil.

Operation ICEBERG: The code name for the invasion of Okinawa.

Operational Requirements: The needs of the troops in an operation.

Pacific Ocean Areas (POA): A military command responsible for planning and conducting operations in the Pacific Ocean.

PAC-AID: An agreement between the different military commands in the Pacific.

Palau: A group of islands in the western Pacific Ocean, south of the Mariana Islands and north of New Guinea.

PB: "Patrol Bomber"

PB(HL): "Patrol Bomber (Heavy, Long Range)"

PB(MIS): "Patrol Bomber (Medium, Seaplane)"

PC: "Patrol Craft".

PC-PS: "Patrol Craft - Submarine Chaser"

Photo: "Photograph"

Photo Reconnaissance: The use of aircraft to take photographs of enemy territory for intelligence purposes.

Photographic Reconnaissance Squadron: A squadron of aircraft that is equipped to take photographs of enemy territory.

PT: "Patrol Torpedo" boat. Small, fast torpedo boats used to patrol waters, primarily in harbors or to attack enemy ships.

Phase I: The initial part of Operation ICEBERG, focused on capturing the southern part of OKINAWA and establishing a base there.

Phase II: The second phase of Operation ICEBERG, focusing on capturing the rest of OKINAWA and the island of IE SHIMA.

Phase III: The third phase of Operation ICEBERG, focusing on capturing additional islands to further extend the U.S. blockade and bombardment of Japan.

PhibsPac: "Amphibious Forces, Pacific Fleet"

POA: "Pacific Ocean Areas"

Potable Water: Safe drinking water.

Pre-embarkation Unit: A unit that is responsible for preparing troops and equipment for embarkation on ships.

Preliminary Bombardment: Bombardment that is conducted in advance of a landing to soften enemy defenses.

Preliminary Reconnaissance: Reconnaissance that is conducted before an operation to gather intelligence about the enemy and the terrain.

Prescribed Stocks: The amount of supplies that are considered necessary to support an operation.

Prisoner of war (POW): A member of an enemy military force who is captured during combat.

Proposed Assignment: A plan for how units will be assigned to different tasks.

Proposed Assembly: A plan for how units will be grouped together in advance of an operation.

Proposed Approach: A plan for how ships will approach an objective.

Proposed Fast Carrier Operations: A plan for how fast carrier task forces will be used to support an operation.

Proposed Shore Based Air Operations: A plan for how air units based ashore will be used to support an operation.

Ration: A fixed amount of food that is provided to troops.

RCT: "Regimental Combat Team"

Rehearsals: Practice runs of an operation that are conducted to train the troops and work out any problems in the plan.

Relief: A unit that is sent to replace another unit in an operation.

Repatriate: To return an individual or group of individuals to their home country.

Resupply: To provide additional supplies to a unit.

Reserve: A force of troops or equipment that is not committed to an operation but is held ready to deploy as needed.

Rescron: A type of seaplane.

Revets: A type of cover that is built over military vehicles and equipment to protect them from attack.

R. E. KEETON: Assistant Flag Secretary, U.S. Pacific Fleet.

R:.:EOSA: "Republic of China", referring to Taiwan.

RYUKYUS: The Ryukyu Islands, located to the south of Japan.

RYUETKYUS: "Ryukyu Islands"

SAIPAN: A large island in the Mariana Islands.

Sakashima GUNTO: "Sakishima Islands". A group of islands in the southern Ryukyus.

SAN FRANCISCO: A city located on the west coast of the United States.

SAR: "Search and Rescue"

SASEBO: A major naval base located in Japan.

S/L: "Searchlight"

Scheme of Maneuver: A plan for how troops will move during an operation.

Schouten Islands: A group of islands located off the coast of New Guinea.

Sea approaches: The waters that lead to a coastline or island.

Seaplane: An aircraft that is designed to land and take off on water.

Seaplane Base: A base for seaplanes.

Service: Used to describe military units or ships that support combat units, such as medical units, supply units, and transport units.

Service Squadron: A squadron of ships that is responsible for providing support services to other ships.

Service Troops: Troops that are responsible for supporting combat units.

SHANGHAI: A city in China.

SHANTUNG: A province in China.

SHIMONOSDKI: A port city in Japan.

SHIMA: "Island"

SHIMDJI: An island near MIYAKO JIMA.

SHITOOKE: A location on the northeast coast of KIKAI JIMA.

SHURI: A city on the island of OKINAWA.

South China Sea: A sea located to the south of China, east of Vietnam.

SoPac: "South Pacific Area". A military command responsible for planning and conducting operations in the South Pacific.

Southern KYUSHU: The southern part of KYUSHU, the main island of Japan.

Southwest Pacific Area (SWPA): A military command responsible for planning and conducting operations in the Southwest Pacific.

Squadron: A military unit composed of several smaller units, such as companies.

Standard Landing Craft Unit (SLCU): A group of landing craft.

Strategic: Used to describe actions or targets that are of high importance to the overall outcome of a war.

Strategic Air Force (POA): A military command responsible for conducting long-range bombing missions against strategic targets.

Strategic Support: Support that is provided to an operation that is of high importance to the overall outcome of a war.

Strike: An air or naval attack on a target.

Strike Bombers: Bomber aircraft that are designed to attack targets on the ground or at sea.

Submarine: A warship that is designed to operate underwater.

Submarine Chaser: A small, fast warship that was used to hunt submarines.

Surface Radar: A type of radar that is mounted on ships and used to detect enemy ships and aircraft.

Surface Vessel: A ship that operates on the surface of the water, as opposed to submarines.

Supplementary Military Yen: A type of currency that was issued by the U.S. military during World War II to be used in occupied territories.

Support: To provide assistance to an operation.

Support Shipping: Ships that are used to transport supplies and equipment to troops in an operation.

Sustained: Used to describe a long-lasting or ongoing operation. For example, the authors of this document refer to "sustained strikes", meaning strikes that are repeated over a long period.

Tactical: Used to describe actions or targets that are of importance to a specific battle.

Tactical Air Force: A military command responsible for conducting air operations in support of ground troops.

Tactical Support: Support that is provided to an operation that is of importance to a specific battle.

Tank: A heavily armored vehicle equipped with a large gun.

Tank Bn: "Tank Battalion".

Tank Regiment: A military unit composed of several tank battalions.

Target: A military objective that is to be attacked.

Task Force: A group of military units that are assigned to a specific mission.

Tasks: The missions or objectives of an operation.

Tenth Army: A U.S. Army command that was responsible for operations in the Pacific.

TFJ: "Task Force, Japan". The task force composed of the units that will attack Japan.

T-Day: A day in a future operation.

Tender Based: Describes an aircraft that is based on a tender ship, such as a seaplane tender or a carrier tender.

Tenth Army Headquarters: The command headquarters for the Tenth Army.

Terrain: The physical features of a region, such as mountains, valleys, rivers, and forests.

Topographic: Relating to the physical features of a region.

Torpedo: A self-propelled explosive weapon that is used to sink ships.

Torpedo Bomber: A bomber aircraft that is equipped to launch torpedoes.

Torpedo Net: A type of net that is used to prevent enemy torpedoes from reaching a ship or harbor.

TransRon: "Transport Squadron". A squadron of ships that are used to transport troops and equipment.

Transport: To move troops or equipment from one location to another, typically by ship or aircraft.

Transport Carrier: A carrier that is designed to transport troops, equipment, and supplies.

Troop Capy: "Troop Capacity". A measure of how many troops a ship can carry.

Troop List: A list of the troops that are assigned to an operation.

Truk: An atoll in the Caroline Islands.

TSUKEN JIMA: An island located off the eastern coast of OKINAWA.

U.S. The United States of America.

ULITHi: An atoll in the western Pacific Ocean.

Underwater Detection: The process of detecting enemy submarines using sonar, hydrophones, or other means.

Underwater Detection Gear: Equipment, such as sonar or hydrophones, that is used to detect enemy submarines.

Units of Fire: A measure of the amount of ammunition that a unit can fire.

Unit: A military organization, such as a company, battalion, regiment, or division.

Utility Towing Squadron: A squadron of aircraft that is responsible for towing targets and other equipment.

VLR: "Very Long Range"

VMF: "Marine Fighter Squadron"

VMF(N): "Marine Night Fighter Squadron"

VMTB: "Marine Torpedo Bomber Squadron"

VBM: "Marine Bomber Squadron"

VBH: "Heavy Bomber Squadron"

VD: "Photographic Squadron"

VF: "Fighter Squadron"

VF(N): "Night Fighter Squadron"

VLADIVOSTOK: A city located on the Russian side of the Pacific Ocean.

Voyage Repairs: Repairs that are made to a ship after it has completed a long voyage.

WAN: "Harbor"

W-Day: The day when Phase II of Operation ICEBERG is to be completed.

War Department: The department of the U.S. Government responsible for the military.

West Coast: The western coast of the United States.

White Gas: A type of gasoline that is used in stoves and lanterns.

Wing: A large military unit composed of several groups.

WW: "World War"

Y-JIMA: "Island"

YANGTZE: A large river in China.

YERABU: An island near MIYAKO JIMA.

YMS: "Minesweeper"

YONABAPRU: A location on the southern end of OKINAWA.

YONTAN: A location on the southern end of OKINAWA.

YONABL,RU: A location on the southern end of OKINAWA.

YOKOHAMA: A major port city in Japan.

YOKUi: "Yokohama"

YOG: "Oil-er"

YMT: "Motor Torpedo" boat. A type of PT boat.

YO: "Utility Boat"

YP: "Patrol Boat"

YTP: "Typewriter Repair Unit"

Z': "Zero". A Japanese fighter aircraft.

Zone: A designated area, typically in the ocean.

Zone Notices: Notices that are issued to ships and aircraft to warn them of dangers or restrictions in a specific zone.

Please note that this glossary is meant to be helpful to a lay reader. It does not include all of the terms used in the document, and it is not a substitute for a professional dictionary or encyclopedia.

Timeline

December 28, 1944: Transport Squadron I departs Lingayen for the Marianas empty.

January 4, 1945: Transport Squadron I arrives in the Marianas after a 1,800 mile voyage.

January 6, 1945: Transport Squadron II departs Lingayen for New Guinea with casualties.

January 10, 1945: Transport Squadron III departs Lingayen on a second trip to New Guinea.

January 13, 1945: Transport Squadron II arrives in New Guinea after a 2,000 mile voyage.

January 17, 1945: Transport Squadron III arrives in Leyte after a 950 mile voyage.

January 18, 1945: Transport Squadron VIII departs Pearl Harbor for New Caledonia.

January 20, 1945: Transport Squadron III departs Lingayen on a second trip. Transport Squadron I completes loading of the 3rd Marine Division in preparation for detachment. Transport Squadron II completes unloading in New Guinea.

January 22, 1945: Transport Squadron VII departs Pearl Harbor for Guadalcanal.

January 23, 1945: Transport Squadron I arrives at Iwo Jima after a 780 mile voyage.

January 25, 1945: Transport Squadron III completes interim upkeep in Leyte. Transport Squadron IV completes interim upkeep in Leyte.

January 27, 1945: Transport Squadron V departs Iwo Jima for Saipan with casualties.

January 30, 1945: Transport Squadron V arrives in Saipan. Group B departs Iwo Jima for Leyte.

January 31, 1945: Transport Squadron VIII arrives in New Caledonia.

February 2, 1945: Group B arrives in Leyte. Group A departs Iwo Jima for Ulithi.

February 3, 1945: Transport Squadron VII completes voyage repairs in Guadalcanal.

February 5, 1945: Group A arrives in Ulithi.

February 7, 1945: Transport Squadron VII completes rehearsals for the 1st Marine Division.

February 9, 1945: Transport Squadron VIII completes rehearsals for the 77th Division.

February 10, 1945: Transport Squadron VI departs Iwo Jima for the Marianas with one combat division.

February 12, 1945: Transport Squadron IV completes rehearsals for the 96th Division. Transport Squadron III completes rehearsals for the 7th Division.

February 13, 1945: Transport Squadron VI arrives in the Marianas. Transport Squadron VII completes loading. Transport Squadron VIII completes loading. Transport Squadron II completes rehearsals for the 6th Marine Division.

February 15, 1945: Transport Squadron VIII arrives in Okinawa. Transport Squadron VII arrives in Okinawa. Transport Squadron II departs Guadalcanal for Okinawa.

February 16, 1945: Transport Squadron I departs the Marianas after completing unloading.

February 18, 1945: Transport Squadron VI departs the Marianas for Espiritu Santo. Transport Squadron V completes rehearsals for the 2nd Marine Division.

February 19, 1945: Transport Squadron II arrives in Okinawa. Group C departs Guadalcanal for Okinawa. Group A departs Ulithi for Okinawa. Transport Squadron V departs Saipan for Okinawa. Transport Squadron I arrives in the Marianas.

February 21, 1945: Transport Squadron VI arrives in Espiritu Santo after a 2,250 mile voyage.

February 23, 1945: Group A arrives in Okinawa.

February 24, 1945: Transport Squadron V arrives in Okinawa. Group B departs Leyte for Okinawa.

February 25, 1945: Transport Squadron IV arrives in Okinawa. Transport Squadron III arrives in Okinawa.

February 26, 1945: Transport Squadron VI completes interim upkeep at Espiritu Santo.

February 28, 1945: Group B arrives in Okinawa. Group C arrives in Okinawa.

March 1, 1945: Transport Squadron I arrives in Okinawa after completing unloading. Transport Squadron II arrives in Okinawa after completing unloading. Transport Squadron IV arrives in Okinawa after completing unloading. Transport Squadron III arrives in Okinawa after completing unloading.

March 8, 1945: Transport Squadron VI completes interim upkeep at Espiritu Santo and is available to load the 27th Division for service in the ICEBERG operation.

Index of Places

UNCLASSIFIED

SECRET

SECRET

UNCLASSIFIED

Report Documentation Page

Form Approved
OMB No. 0704-0188

Public reporting burden for the collection of information is estimated to average 1 hour per response, including the time for reviewing instructions, searching existing data sources, gathering and maintaining the data needed, and completing and reviewing the collection of information. Send comments regarding this burden estimate or any other aspect of this collection of information, including suggestions for reducing this burden, to Washington Headquarters Services, Directorate for Information Operations and Reports, 1215 Jefferson Davis Highway, Suite 1204, Arlington VA 22202-4302. Respondents should be aware that notwithstanding any other provision of law, no person shall be subject to a penalty for failing to comply with a collection of information if it does not display a currently valid OMB control number.

1. REPORT DATE	2. REPORT TYPE	3. DATES COVERED
DEC 1944	**N/A**	-

4. TITLE AND SUBTITLE	5a. CONTRACT NUMBER
U. S. Pacific Fleet And Pacific Ocean Areas Joint Staff Study, ICEBERG Operation	5b. GRANT NUMBER
	5c. PROGRAM ELEMENT NUMBER

6. AUTHOR(S)	5d. PROJECT NUMBER
	5e. TASK NUMBER
	5f. WORK UNIT NUMBER

7. PERFORMING ORGANIZATION NAME(S) AND ADDRESS(ES)	8. PERFORMING ORGANIZATION REPORT NUMBER
Headquarters United States Pacific Fleet And Pacific Ocean Areas	

9. SPONSORING/MONITORING AGENCY NAME(S) AND ADDRESS(ES)	10. SPONSOR/MONITOR'S ACRONYM(S)
	11. SPONSOR/MONITOR'S REPORT NUMBER(S)

12. DISTRIBUTION/AVAILABILITY STATEMENT
Approved for public release, distribution unlimited

13. SUPPLEMENTARY NOTES
JFSC WWII Declassified Records.

14. ABSTRACT

15. SUBJECT TERMS

16. SECURITY CLASSIFICATION OF:			17. LIMITATION OF ABSTRACT	18. NUMBER OF PAGES	19a. NAME OF RESPONSIBLE PERSON
a. REPORT	b. ABSTRACT	c. THIS PAGE			
unclassified	**unclassified**	**unclassified**	**SAR**	**185**	

Standard Form 298 (Rev. 8-98)
Prescribed by ANSI Std Z39-18

JOINT STAFF STUDY

ICEBERG

28700

CinCPac File

A16

U. S.
UNITED STATES PACIFIC FLEET
AND PACIFIC OCEAN AREAS.
Headquarters of the Commander in Chief

Serial 0001063

Change address 12/8/44
- 16 M.R.

UNCLASSIFIED

2 December 1944

From:	Commander in Chief, U.S. Pacific Fleet and Pacific Ocean Areas.
To :	Distribution List.
Subject:	Joint Staff Study, ICEBERG Operation.
Reference:	(a) Subject Staff Study, CinCPOA ser. 000131 of 25 October 1944.
Enclosures:	(A) Paragraph 2 k, of Appendix E to subject study - "Military Government".
	(B) Paragraph 5 d, of Appendix E to subject study - "Care of Civilians".

1.   Reference (a) states that discussion of Military Government and Care of Civilians in subject operation will be issued separately at a later date.

2.   Forwarded herewith as Enclosure (A) is a discussion of Military Government to be included as paragraph 2 k in subject staff study. Also forwarded as Enclosure (B) is a discussion of Care of Civilians to be included as paragraph 5 d of subject staff study.

J.H. TOWERS
Deputy CinCPac & CinCPOA

DISTRIBUTION LIST

CominCh	(12)
CNO	(2)
Com5thFlt	(12)
ComGen10thArmy	(25)
ComPhibsPac	(8)
Com5thPhibFor	(20)
ComGenPOA	(15)
Com3rdFlt	(2)
ComGenFMFPac	(10)
ComAirPac	(4)
ComGenAirFMFPac	(2)
ComFwdAreaCentPac	(4)
ComGenAAFPOA	(5)
ComServPac	(2)
ComSoPac	(2)
CinCSWPA	(2)
Com7thFlt	(1)

28700

Indexed

O.L.THORNE
Flag Secretary.

DECLASSIFIED IAW DOD MEMO OF 3 MAY 1972, SUBJ:,
DECLASSIFICATION OF WWII RECORDS.   JAN 18 '77

UNCLASSIFIED

A16/Ice

UNITED STATES PACIFIC FLEET
AND PACIFIC OCEAN AREAS
Headquarters of the Commander in Chief

Serial   000131   25 October 1944.

ICEBERG

1.   The attached study of ICEBERG is the basis for
directives for the operation but is not in itself a directive
or considered to commit the Commander in Chief, U. S. Pacific
Fleet and Pacific Ocean Areas to any course of action. It is
circulated to Joint Staff and major subordinate commanders to
facilitate planning and implementation, both operational and
logistic.

2.   Changes may be made in the study as the situation develops.

                                FORREST SHERMAN,
                                Deputy Chief of Staff.

DISTRIBUTION:

                              Copy No.

Cominch(12)..................   1-12 incl.
CNO (2)...................... 13-14
Com5thFlt (12)............... 15-26 incl.
ComGen 10thArmy (25)........ 27-51 incl.
ComPhibsPac (8).............. 52-59 incl.
Com5thPhibFor (20)........... 60-79 incl.
ComGenPOA (15)............... 80-94 incl.
Com3rdFlt (2)................ 95-96
ComGenFMFPac (10)............ 97-106 incl.
ComAirPac (4)................ 107-110 incl.
ComGenAirFMFPac (2)......... 111-112
ComFwdAreaCentPac (4)....... 113-116 incl.
ComGenAAFPOA (5)............ 117-121 incl.
ComServPac (2).............. 122-123
ComSoPac (2)................ 124-125
CinCSWPA (2)................ 126-127
Com7thFlt (1)...............   128

28700

      O. L. THORNE,
      Flag Secretary.

Pac-12-eiw

ICEBERG

Table of Contents

CONCEPT

Pac-12-wmh   ICEBERG

                                    CONCEPT

I.   DIRECTIVE

      The Joint Chiefs of Staff have directed the Commander
in Chief Pacific Ocean Areas to occupy one or more positions
in the NANSEI SHOTO, target date 1 March 1945.

II.   ASSUMPTIONS

      That the seizure of IWO JIMA is completed at a
sufficiently early date to permit availability of fire
support units and close air support units for the assault
in the NANSEI SHOTO.

      That results of our operations against the EMPIRE,
FORMOSA, the RYUKYUS, and the enemy Fleet during the period
preceding the target date for the NANSEI SHOTO assault indicates that we will be able to maintain continuing control
of the air in the objective area.

      That assault shipping and supporting naval forces
are released promptly from LUZON operations.

III. PURPOSES

      To establish bases from which to:

            (1) Attack the main islands of JAPAN and their
sea approaches with naval and air forces.

            (2) Support further operations in the regions
bordering on the EAST CHINA SEA.

            (3) Sever Japanese sea and air communications
between the EMPIRE and the mainland of ASIA, FORMOSA,
MALAYA, and the NETHERLANDS EAST INDIES.

                          -1-

To establish secure sea and air communications through the EAST CHINA SEA to the coast of CHINA and the YANGTZE VALLEY.

To maintain unremitting military pressure against JAPAN.

IV.   TASKS

Immediate:

Capture, occupy, defend, and develop OKINAWA Island and establish control of the sea and air in the NANSEI SHOTO area.

Eventual:

Extend control of the NANSEI SHOTO by capturing, occupying, defending and developing additional positions.

V.   CONCEPT OF OPERATIONS

Carrier attacks on JAPAN and the air threat from the MARIANAS together with our seizure of IWO JIMA are expected to force a concentration of Japanese air strength in the heart of the EMPIRE. Our Expeditionary Forces will be subject to strong attacks by Japanese aviation staged through KYUSHU or the CHINA Coast and FORMOSA.

By making powerful air attacks on the EMPIRE and FORMOSA prior to the OKINAWA assault we can inflict heavy losses upon Japanese air forces and reduce the potential threat to our expeditionary forces.

The capture and occupation of the OKINAWA Islands require that our forces establish undisputed control of the sea and air in the area of operations. Accordingly, the movement into the RYUKYUS will be preceded by air operations as follows:

(1) Preliminary reconnaissance of the objectives by air forces based on the Asiatic mainland and by those based in the MARIANAS.

(2) Destructive attacks on the main Japanese islands by carrier aircraft and by very long range bombers operating from CHINA and the MARIANAS.

(3) Destructive attacks on the Japanese air forces and bases in FORMOSA, AMOY, and the PESCADORES by carrier task forces and by air forces based in LUZON.

Prior to amphibious operations against OKINAWA, strong carrier attacks will be made as necessary against critical objectives in FORMOSA, the main Japanese islands, and in the RYUKYUS in order to destroy enemy forces and installations.

In advance of the operations, the sea communications of the RYUKYUS will be destroyed to the maximum extent practicable by the action of submarines and by surface and air attacks on shipping.

The approach of the attack force will be covered by further intensified attacks on enemy air bases in FORMOSA, KYUSHU and on islands of the NANSEI SHOTO.

The scheme of maneuver will be designed to gain early use of sufficient airdrome capacity in OKINAWA, together with unloading facilities adequate to support its development, to maintain positive control of the air in the area.

Air bases will be activated rapidly to support the air garrison listed under Forces Required. The air force to be based ashore will total approximately 650 airplanes.

The port of NAHA will be developed to its maximum capacity to accommodate support shipping and to support forces for subsequent operations. NAKAGUSUKU BAY will be developed as an advanced fleet base with port facilities to provide logistic support for major fleet units and occupation forces.

Following is the general sequence of operations in NANSEI SHOTO:

Phase I Capture the southern portion of OKINAWA including small adjacent islands and develop base facilities.

Phase II Seize the remainder of OKINAWA and IE SHIMA and develop additional necessary base facilities in favorable localities.

Phase III Exploit our position in the NANSEI SHOTO seizing and developing additional positions with forces locally available.

VI FORCES

a. Ground Forces.

Tenth Army Headquarters and Army troops.

CORPS	PRINCIPAL TROOPS	MOUNTING AREAS
III Amphibious Corps	1st MarDiv	RUSSELLS

- 4 -

Pac-12-wmh

~~REGRADED~~

CORPS	PRINCIPAL TROOPS	MOUNTING AREAS
	2nd MarDiv	SAIPAN
	6th MarDiv	GUADALCANAL
XXIV Army Corps	7th Infantry Division	LEYTE
	96th Infantry Division	LEYTE
	77th Infantry Division	NEW CALEDONIA

In area reserve:

27th Infantry Division at ESPIRITU SANTO.

One infantry division to be designated, mounted

in the South Pacific.

b. Garrison Air Forces

4 Groups Marine Fighters	288 VMF
2 Squadrons Marine Night fighters	24 VMF(N)
2 Squadrons Marine torpedo bombers	36 VMTB
2 Squadrons Navy heavy patrol bombers	24 PB(HL)
1 Squadron Navy photographic	6 VD
1 Squadron photo-reconnaissance (P-38)	12 F-5
2 Groups Army medium bombers	128 B-25
2 Groups Army heavy bombers	96 B-24
2 Squadrons Navy Medium seaplanes	24 PB(MS)

See Appendix F for detailed list of Garrison and Service Units.

c. NAVAL FORCES

(1) Assault

8 BB		24 DMS	
9 OBB		36 LCI(G)	
11 CV		12 LCI(M)	
7 CVL		18 LCI(L)	

- 5 -

Pac-12-wmh

18	CVE(combatant)	20	LCT
1	CB	6	ATF
12	CA	2	ATR
10	CL	1	AKN
4	CL(AA)	4	AN
158	DD	48	PC-PCS-SC
48	DE	24	YMS
8	AGC	1500	LVT (cargo)
12	DM	300	LVT (tank)
24	AM	800	DUKW

		Troop Capy	Cargo Capy (MT)
90	APA (AP-APH-LVS)	117,000	90,000
36	AKA (AK)	5,400	108,000
8	LSD	1,600	8,000
150	LST	30,000	75,000
60	LSM	4,500	12,000
16	APD	2,200	
		160,700	293,000

(2) <u>For Area Reserve</u>

To be deployed at mounting points by D-Day and to be additional to naval forces allocated for the initial assault.

1 AGC

12 PC-PCS-SC

12 DE

- 6 -

		Troop Capy	Cargo Capy (MT)
30	APA(AP)	39,000	30,000
12	AKA(AK)	1,800	36,000
20	LCT	4,000	10,000
10	LSM	750	2,000
	Totals	45,550	78,000

(3) Garrison

Base Supported

The following naval craft, to be obtained from assault forces where possible, are expected to be based at OKINAWA and will require logistic support from the base:

20 LCT	200 LCM	150 LCVP	24 PT
2 YMT	6 YO		2 YNg
2 YOG	4 YHB	2 YP	

Fleet Supported.

The following additional naval craft, to be obtained from assault forces where possible, will be required for the support and defense of the base, and will be supported from fleet sources:

18 DD	8 ATF	1 ARL	4 AM	1 ARB
6 DE	10 LST	1 AD	4 AN	1 ARS
18 PC-PCS SC	18 LCI(L)	1 AGP	1 AVR	1 AVD
6 YMS	18 LCI(G)	1 ARD	1 AV	2 AVP

d. Summary of Forces (See Appendix F for details)

	Combat	Service	Totals
ARMY	95,811	47,932	143,743
NAVY	2,468	57,281	59,749
MARINE	73,676	10,177	83,853
	171,955	115,390	287,345

Area Reserve 2 Infantry Divisions in SoPac 28,400

004 90 6 1

- 7 -

Iac-122-rr

ICEBERG

APPENDIX   A

GROUND FORCES

1.   ENEMY STRENGTH AND CAPABILITIES.

The estimated strength of the Japanese Forces in the
OKINAWA Group, as of 15 October 1944 is 48,600, including:

1 Army headquarters	750
2 First line infantry divisions	35,000
1 Fortress group (Possibly an independent mixed brigade)	4,500
Naval personnel	2,100
Air Base personnel	1,500
Shipping engineer personnel	2,500
1 Tank regiment (30 L, 47 M tanks)	750
Construction personnel	1,500
Total	48,600

An additional first line division (less 1 regt) is estimated to
be on MIYAKO JIMA, 150 miles SW of OKINAWA JIMA; the excepted
regiment is estimated to be in the DAITO Group, 170 miles east
of OKINAWA JIMA. A fourth division is estimated to be in the
AMAMI O SHIMA Group, 90 miles northeast of OKINAWA JIMA. Reinforcement of th. NANSEI SHOTO was initiated in July 1944, at
which time the two divisions arrived at OKINAWA JIMA. By target
date these divisions will have had over seven months in which to
organize for defense. As a result of the capture of LUZON and
IWO JIMA, the Japanese will probably exert maximum effort to
complete full defensive preparations in the NANSEI SHOTO.

The civil population of 443,000, three-quarters of whom
live in the southern half of OKINAWA JIMA, offers a potential
source for homeguard, milita, and guerilla forces who in them-

selves constitute a serious threat of opposition.

From previous experience it is known that the Japanese will resist fanatically any invasion of the NANSEI SHOTO, and will counterattack and reinforce within the limits imposed by our superior air and naval forces.

Information as to enemy defensive installations on OKINAWA JIMA is meager, but there are indications that the southern half of the island (south of a general line from SERAKAKI to CHIMU) will contain the bulk of garrison forces, and have strongly organized defenses at the beaches and in depth. The northern half of the island is mountainous with a high central ridge bordered by tarraces. Therefore, it is assumed that, with the exception of MOTOBU Peninsula, the Japanese will defend this area lightly. IE SHIMA is fortified, and is the location of an excellent airfield. The NAHA Harbor area is reported to be defended by coast defense guns installed on the high ground south of NAHA. These guns are capable of opposing amphibious assault within their range on the east as well as on the west coast. The areas guarding the approaches to NAKAGUSUKU WAN and CHIMU WAN, including the small satellite islands off the east coast, are reported to be heavily fortified. Five airfields are situated in the southern half of OKINAWA JIMA, - two in the JINA-KATENA area, two in the NAHA area, and one on the east coast midway between KATENA and NAHA. These fields are expected to be strongly defended.

Information on landing beaches is sketchy although locations of fifteen are known on the southern half of OKINAWA JIMA; of these, ten are on the west coast, one on the southeast, and four

Pac-122-rr

~~TOP SECRET~~

on the east. Further reconnaissance will probably reveal other
suitable beaches. There is at least one landing beach on each
satellite island off the east coast. Fringing reefs are found
off all beaches.

According to available information, the most favorable
coastline for landing and for advance inland is west of KATENA,
north and south of the river mouth.

2.   ASSAULT FORCES REQUIRED

The strength of the forces required for the seizure and
occupation of OKINAWA JIMA is estimated to be an army of two
corps of three reinforced divisions each in the assault, with
two Army divisions in area reserve.

Units of the XXIV Corps will be mounted in LEYTE and NEW
CALEDONIA. Rehearsals will take place in the mounting areas.

Units of the III Amphibious Corps, less one division, will
be mounted in the GUADALCANAL - RUSSELLS area and rehearsed in
the GUADALCANAL area. The 2nd Marine Division will be mounted
in the MARIANAS and will be the third division of this Corps.

Two Army divisions, the 27th at ESPIRITU SANTO, and an
additional division to be designated, will constitute the
area reserve.

3.   DEFENSE FORCES REQUIRED

OKINAWA JIMA lies within bomber range of FORMOSA, the CHINA
COAST and JAPAN proper and within fighter range of other islands
of the NANSEI SHOTO Group. It can be expected that enemy re-
action to the occupation of this island and any other islands
in the NANSEI SHOTO will be strong in air and surface vessel
counterattack with a possible attempt on the part of the Japanese to retake OKINAWA JIMA. It is estimated that two infantry

~~SECRET~~

divisions taken from the assault force will be required for garrison.

The principle bases requiring antiaircraft protection will be NAHA, BATEN KO, YONABARU, KUBA SAKI, ONO MISAKI, KOGUSUKU, OSUNOHANA, CHIMU, and TSUKEN JIMA. It is contemplated that eight airfields will be activated in the southern half of OKINAWA JIMA and a seaplane base on TSUKEN JIMA. In order to provide the necessary anti-aircraft artillery protection for installations on OKINAWA JIMA five Army AAA gun battalions, five Army AAA automatic weapons battalions, two Army AAA searchlight battalions and four Marine anti-aircraft battalions will be required.

Coast defenses are required for the protection of the Port of NAHA, the naval base of NAKAGUSUKU WAN and the seaplane base of TSUKEN JIMA. Three Army 155-mm gun battalions of seacoast artillery (SM) will be required.

4. SCHEME OF MANEUVER

The scheme of maneuver for operations against the NANSEI SHOTO will comprise three phases, as follows:

PHASE I. See Annex 1

The southern half of OKINAWA JIMA (that part south of a general line from SERAKAKI to CHIMU), including the satellite islands off the east coast, has been selected as the objective area for this phase. The scheme of maneuver is designed to isolate the objective area by seizing ISHIKAWI Isthmus in order to prevent enemy reinforcement from the north. Simultaneously the assault forces will seize and occupy a general east-west line from KUBA SAKI in order to prevent enemy reinforcement from the south. After capture and occupation of the northern half of the objective area, the attack is continued to capture

- 11 -

and occupy the remainder of the objective area.

PHASE II. See Annex 1.

This phase comprises the capture and occupation of the remainder of OKINAWA JIMA and of IE SHIMA. It will be initiated upon completion of PHASE I on W-Day to be announced by the Commanding General Expeditionary Troops. The seizure of these objectives will be accomplished by a shore-to-shore amphibious assault on IE SHIMA, and a combined shore-to-shore amphibious and land assault against the north half of OKINAWA JIMA. Forces locally available will execute the operation. The scheme of maneuver should embrace the early capture of MOTOBU Peninsula, followed by the capture of IE SHIMA, followed by capture of the remainder of OKINAWA JIMA.

PHASE III

This phase will comprise the seizure and occupation of other positions in the NANSEI SHOTO as directed by CinCPOA.

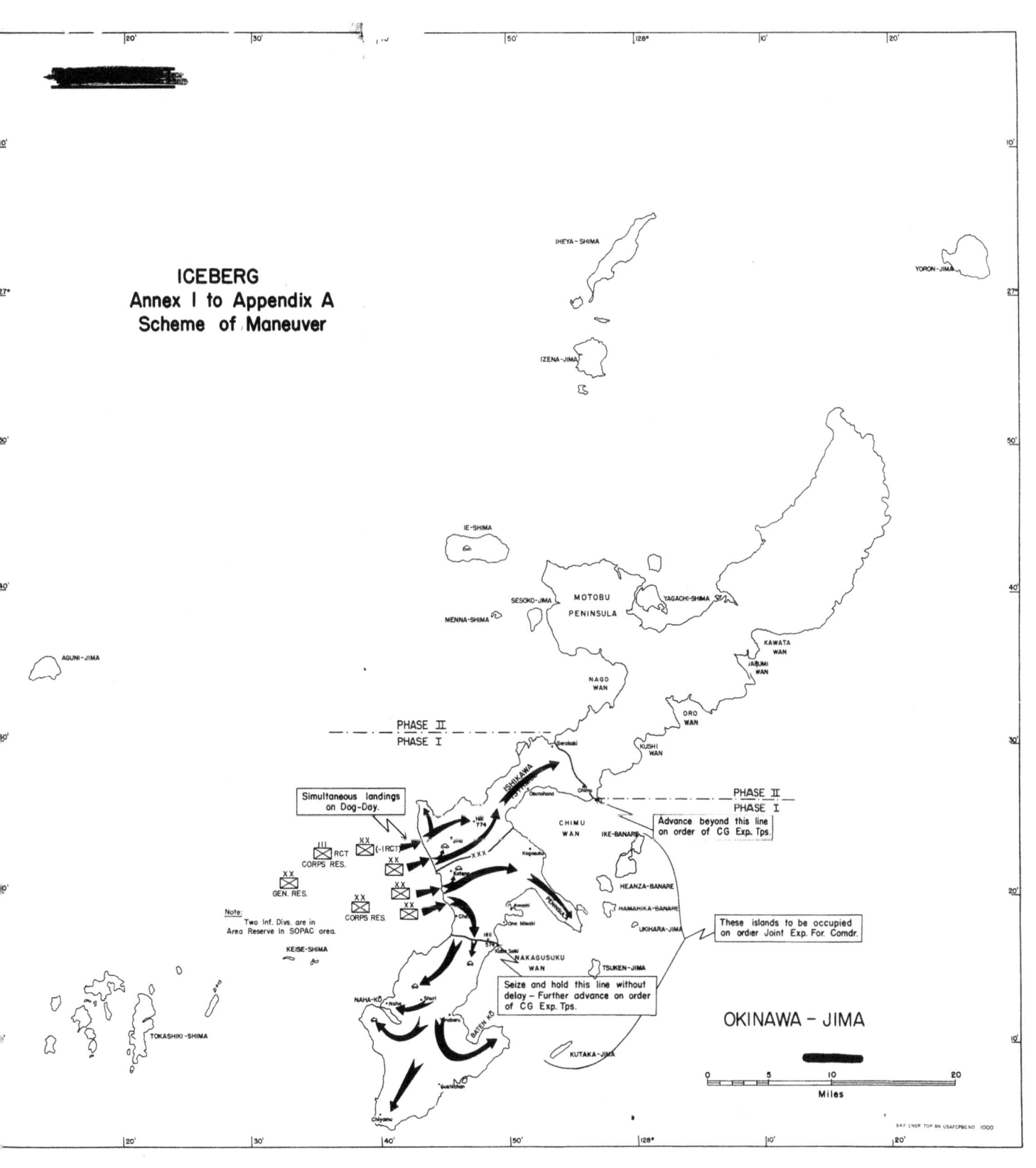

ICEBERG
Annex I to Appendix A
Scheme of Maneuver

OKINAWA - JIMA

Pac-123/125-jh

ICEBERG

APPENDIX B

AIR FORCES

1. CONCEPT OF OPERATIONS.

Preliminary air bombardment of FORMOSA and OKINAWA will be conducted by the Far Eastern Air Force and 20th Air Force from bases in LUZON, CHINA, and the MARIANAS to the extent that execution of their primary mission permits.

Air operations in direct preparation for the assault will consist of a series of carrier based attacks on FORMOSA, the NANSEI SHOTO, and the KYUSHU - WESTERN HONSHU area, in that order, to destroy enemy air effectiveness at the objective and supporting bases. This succession of attacks will culminate in a sustained attack on KYUSHU just prior to the assault on OKINAWA.

Air opposition having been eliminated by carrier strikes, replenishment of enemy air bases will be prevented by shore based attacks on FORMOSA and the southern RYUKYUS by aircraft based in LUZON and CHINA, and by continued action of fast carrier groups on KYUSHU and the northern islands of NANSEI SHOTO.

Escort carriers will maintain control of the air at OKINAWA and provide direct air support for the assault.

Very heavy bombers from the MARIANAS will provide general support by continuing operations against targets in the EMPIRE and by heavy attacks on OKINAWA.

Tasks

The tasks to be performed by the air forces are:

(1) Search and reconnaissance.

(2) Destruction of aircraft, aircraft installations and fixed defenses.

- 13 -

(3)   Covering strikes on the EMPIRE.

(4)   Neutralization of enemy bases from which operations in the objective area may be threatened.

(5)   Destruction of enemy naval forces and shipping.

(6)   Close protection of our surface forces.

(7)   Direct air support of landings and operations ashore.

(8)   Air defense of the captured base until garrison air fields are activated.

(9)   Continued neutralization of by-passed enemy bases.

(10) Photographic reconnaissance of objective areas.

2.   OPERATIONS.

   a.   Carrier Forces.

   Fast Carriers   (See Annex 1 to Appendix B)

   The Fast Carrier Task Force will sortie from ULITHI on D-15 and will conduct sustained strikes on the FORMOSA - MIYAKO areas on D-11 and D-10. After fueling and receiving replacements, strikes will be conducted against the OKINAWA - AMAMI O SHIMA areas on D-7, D-6 and D-5. Then after again fueling and receiving replacements strikes will be conducted against the KYUSHU - WESTERN HONSHU areas on D-3, D-2, D-1 and D Days retiring as necessary for fueling.

   Thereafter the Task Groups will rotate in maintaining a covering position and in conducting supporting strikes as necessary for continuing operations.

   During the strikes against OKINAWA on D-7, D-6 and D-5, bombardment by the fast battleships will be conducted.

   Escort Carriers

   The escort carriers will escort and provide air cover for the Expeditionary Force during its movement to the objective and provide direct air support for the assault, occupation and development of the objective as required. Sufficient escort carriers will remain at the objective to provide air defense until garrison airfields are activated.

Transport Carriers

Transport carriers will transport to the area of operations, replacement aircraft, parts, pilots and aircrews for the CVs and CVLs and CVEs. Transport carriers will also transport designated garrison aircraft to the objective.

b. Shore Based Air Forces.

Naval Search Squadrons, POA

Maintain search of ocean areas north and west of the MARIANAS. If development of airfields on IWO JIMA will permit, extend this reconnaissance as far as practicable toward the NANSEI SHOTO and HONSHU when the Fast Carrier Task Force departs from ULITHI on D-15.

Interdict enemy search by offensive patrols from the MARIANAS and IWO JIMA ahead of the Fast Carrier Task Force.

Strategic Air Force, POA

Neutralize enemy bases in the CAROLINES and BONINS. Strike targets of opportunity.

Strike the AMAMI GUNTO and JAPAN as practicable.

Provide fighter escort for VLR attacks on the EMPIRE.

China Based Air Forces.

The 14th Air Force and 20th Bomber Command operations will be coordinated by the Commanding General, CHINA-BURMA-INDIA in conformity with Alternate PAC-AID. Specific operations desired by POA are:

Conduct repeated photographic reconnaissance of OKINAWA.

Beginning D-30 sorties allocated to the support

of POA will be directed against air installations on Northern FORMOSA.

20th Air Force (MARIANAS)

From D-30 to D-8 and D-5 to D Day all sorties which are allocated to the support of ICEBERG will be directed against OKINAWA airfield installations and fixed defenses.

Any sorties which may be scheduled for D-7 and D-6, when the fast carriers are attacking OKINAWA, should be directed against airfields in Southern KYUSHU.

Far Eastern Air Force.

Initiate attacks on enemy air bases in FORMOSA as soon as the situation in LUZON permits.

Maintain neutralization of airfields on FORMOSA and the SAKISHIMA GUNTO following the carrier attacks on these areas.

Maintain search of the SOUTH CHINA SEA, STRAIT OF FORMOSA and the sea areas east of FORMOSA.

3.   COORDINATION.

In accordance with the provisions of Alternate PAC-AID, the Commanding General 14th Air Force will coordinate the operations of the 14th Air Force and of the 20th Bomber Command.

The Commanding General, Strategic Air Force, POA, will coordinate the operations of his command with the 20th Air Force in the MARIANAS.

CinCPOA will coordinate the operations of carrier aviation and all shore based air forces assigned to the Pacific Ocean Areas. He will also coordinate the activities of all air forces under his command with those assigned to other areas.

Pac-123/125-jh

4.   AIR BASE DEVELOPMENT.

Air bases will be developed to accommodate the following air force:

4 groups Marine fighters	288 VMF
2 squadrons Marine night fighters	24 VMF(N)
2 squadrons Marine torpedo bombers	36 VMTB
2 squadrons Navy heavy patrol bombers	24 PB(HL)
1 squadron Navy photographic	6 VD
1 squadron Photo reconnaissance (P-38)	12 F-5
2 groups Army medium bombers	128 B-25
2 groups Army heavy bombers	96 B-24
2 squadrons Medium seaplanes	24 PB(MS)

Eight airfields, four fighter and four bomber, and one seaplane base will adequately support this force.

Operationally, it is desirable that these units be installed as follows:

2 groups VMF	D $\neq$ 5
2 squadrons VMF(N)	D $\neq$ 5

Additional:

2 groups VMF	D $\neq$ 20 or earlier
2 squadrons VMTB	D $\neq$ 20 or earlier
1 group VBM	D $\neq$ 30
1 group VBM	D $\neq$ 40
2 squadrons PB(HL)	D $\neq$ 50
2 groups VBH	D $\neq$ 50
2 squadrons Photo	D $\neq$ 50
2 squadrons PB(MS)(tender based commencing D$\neq$2)	D $\neq$ 60
2 CV groups 200 replacement aircraft	When construction troops available from other airfields.

Subject to adjustments imposed by engineering problems, these units could well be segregated as follows:

4 fighter fields, Marine, each to accommodate 1 VMF group. On each of two of these fields there will be additionally 1 VMF(N) squadron. Provision will also be made for 1 Marine wing headquarters. One of the VMF groups, and one VMF(N) squadron will be located in the southern portion of the island. The remainder of the fighters may be in one general area to the north.

3 Army fields, one for two groups of heavy bombers, the other two each to support one medium bomber group. One photographic reconnaissance squadron will be located on one of these fields.

1 Navy field for 2 VMTB squadrons, 2 PB(HL) squadrons, 1 photographic squadron, plus troop carrier terminal and transient facilities. 1 utility towing squadron and 1 drone squadron when NAKAGUSUKU WAN becomes available as a secure fleet anchorage.

One seaplane base for the operation of 1 squadron of PB(MS) and 1 Rescron and NATS seaplanes.

If terrain studies make a different grouping of units desirable, or permit the use of fewer fields by interlocking dispersal areas, the segregation indicated may be varied.

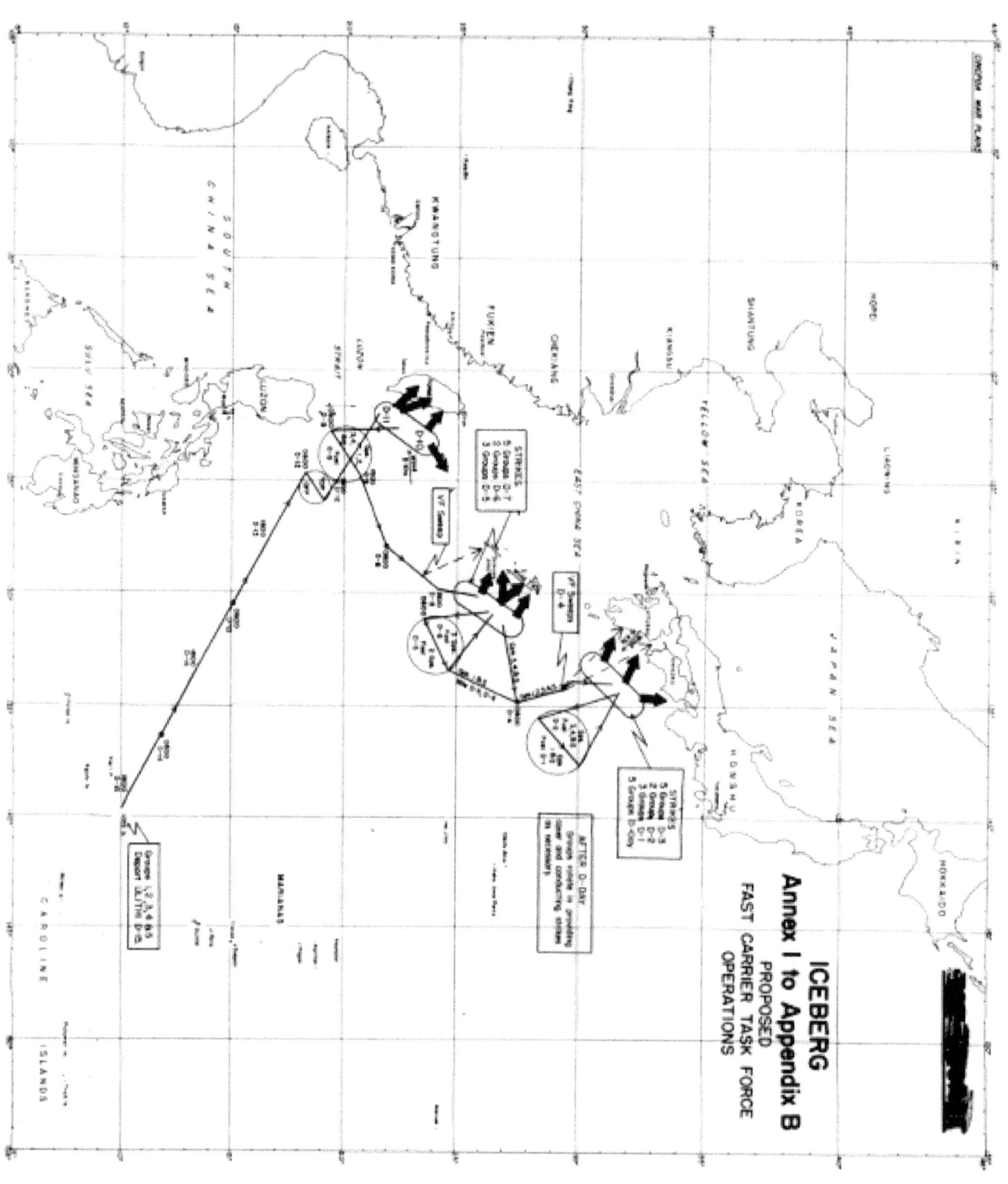

ICEBERG
Annex I to Appendix B
PROPOSED
FAST CARRIER TASK FORCE
OPERATIONS

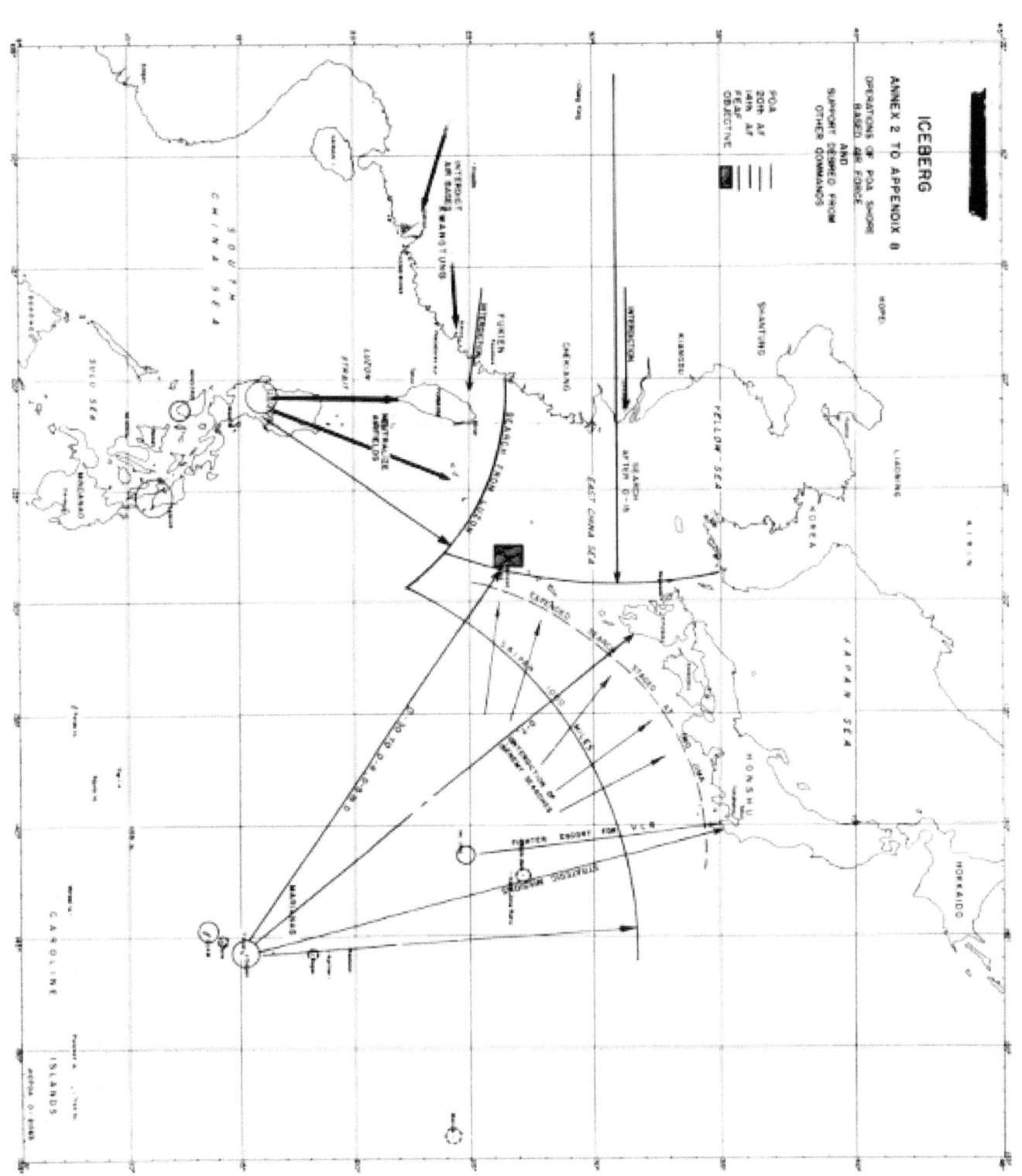

ICEBERG

APPENDIX C

NAVAL FORCES

1. ASSAULT SHIPPING

In order to deploy assault shipping to mount 6 divisions for the assault with 2 additional divisions in reserve, it is planned that ships be provided in the manner indicated in the following table:

	APA(AP-APH-LSV)	AKA(AK)	LST	LSD	LSM	AGC
Assigned 7th Fleet for LINGAYEN	70	19	120	10	30	4
Est. overhaul required after LINGAYEN	10	1	40	2	5	0
To be made available for DETACHMENT from forces employed at LINGAYEN	15	6	0	3	0	0
Remainder available for ICEBERG from LINGAYEN	45	12	80	5	25	4
To be redeployed from DETACHMENT to ICEBERG	15	6	0	3	0	2
To be employed from New Construction and from overhaul to ICEBERG	30	18	70	0	35	1
Total for ICEBERG on D-Day	90	36	150	8	60	7
Additional for ICEBERG reserve to be deployed from DETACHMENT	30	12	20	0	10	1

It is expected that following the landing at LINGAYEN and after selected ships are returned to the West Coast for overhaul, the remaining 60 troop ships (APA-AP-APH-LSV) will be organized in 4 transport squadrons.

These squadrons should adhere approximately to the following operating schedule:

TransRon I	Depart LINGAYEN for MARIANAS empty	Dec. 28
	Arrive MARIANAS (1800 miles)	Jan. 4
	Complete interim upkeep	Jan. 14
	Complete loading 3rd MarDiv for DETACHMENT	Jan. 20
	Arrive IWO JIMA (780 miles)	Jan. 23
	Depart IWO JIMA for MARIANAS with 3rd MarDiv	Feb. 13
	Arrive MARIANAS	Feb. 16
	Complete unloading and depart MARIANAS	Feb. 21
	Arrive SoPac available to load one division as reserve for ICEBERG	Mar. 1
TransRon II	Depart LINGAYEN for NEW GUINEA with Casuals	Jan. 6
	Arrive NEW GUINEA (2000 miles)	Jan. 13
	Complete unloading	Jan. 17
	Arrive GUADALCANAL (900 miles)	Jan. 20
	Complete interim upkeep	Feb. 7
	Complete rehearsals 6th MarDiv	Feb. 13
	Complete final loading and depart	Feb. 19
	Arrive OKINAWA (2870 miles)	Mar. 1
TransRon III	Depart LINGAYEN	Dec. 24
	Arrive NEW GUINEA (2000 miles)	Jan. 3
	Complete unloading and reloading	Jan. 10
	Arrive LINGAYEN (2nd Trip)	Jan. 17
	Depart LINGAYEN	Jan. 22
	Arrive LEYTE (950 miles)	Jan. 25
	Complete interim upkeep	Feb. 12
	Complete rehearsals 7th Div	Feb. 19
	Complete final loading and depart	Feb. 25
	Arrive OKINAWA (1000 miles)	Mar. 1
TransRon IV	Depart LINGAYEN	Dec. 24
	Arrive NEW GUINEA (2000 miles)	Jan. 3
	Complete unloading and reloading	Jan. 10
	Arrive LINGAYEN (2nd Trip)	Jan. 17
	Depart LINGAYEN	Jan. 22
	Arrive LEYTE (950 miles)	Jan. 25
	Complete interim upkeep	Feb. 12
	Complete rehearsals 96th Div.	Feb. 19
	Complete final loading and depart	Feb. 25
	Arrive OKINAWA (1000 miles)	Mar. 1

Pac-12-eiw

In addition to these transport squadrons released from
LINGAYEN, two new squadrons which are to be used in DETACHMENT
should adhere approximately to the following operating schedule:

TransRon V		
	Depart IWO JIMA with Casuals	Jan. 27
	Arrive SAIPAN	Jan. 30
	Complete interim upkeep	Feb. 11
	Complete rehearsals 2nd MarDiv	Feb. 18
	Complete final loading and depart	Feb. 24
	Arrive OKINAWA (1250 miles)	Mar. 1

TransRon VI		
	Depart IWO JIMA with one combat Div.	Feb. 10
	Arrive MARIANAS	Feb. 13
	Complete unloading and depart	Feb. 18
	Arrive ESPIRITU (2250 miles)	Feb. 26
	Complete interim upkeep	Mar. 8
	Available to load 27th Div as reserve for ICEBERG	

In addition to these squadrons, two newly formed squadrons
from new construction will adhere approximately to the following
operating schedule:

TransRon VII		
	Depart PEARL	Jan. 22
	Arrive GUADALCANAL (3200 miles)	Feb. 3
	Complete voyage repairs	Feb. 7
	Complete rehearsals 1st MarDiv	Feb. 13
	Complete final loading	Feb. 19
	Arrive OKINAWA (2870 miles)	Mar. 1

TransRon VIII		
	Depart PEARL	Jan. 18
	Arrive NEW CALEDONIA (3400 miles)	Jan. 31
	Complete voyage repairs	Feb. 3
	Complete rehearsals 77th Div.	Feb. 9
	Complete final loading	Feb. 15
	Arrive OKINAWA (3800 miles)	Mar. 1

2. FIRE SUPPORT GROUPS

It is desirable that the total fire support force be devided into three groups in order to:

(a) Provide fire support during rehearsals for troops mounting in LEYTE and in GUADALCANAL.

(b) Operate in relays at the objective, because the period during which fire support will be required extends over a considerable period of time.

The groups may be organized as follows:

"A"	"B"	"C"
5 OBB	2 OBB	2 OBB
		1 CB
2 CA	2 CA	1 CA
2 CL	1 CL	
9 DD	4 DD	5 DD

Groups should operate in accordance with the following approximate schedule:

Group A	Depart IWO JIMA (DETACHMENT D ≠ 13)	Feb. 2
	Arrive ULITHI	Feb. 5
	Complete interim upkeep rearming, etc.	Feb. 19
	Arrive OKINAWA (ICEBERG D - 6)	Feb. 23
Group B	Depart IWO JIMA (DETACHMENT D≠ 10)	Jan. 30
	Arrive LEYTE	Feb. 2
	Complete upkeep, rearming, rehearsals	Feb. 24
	Arrive OKINAWA (ICEBERG D - 1)	Feb. 28
Group C	Assemble in GUADALCANAL	Jan. 25
	Complete rehearsals etc.	Feb. 19
	Arrive OKINAWA (ICEBERG D - 1)	Feb. 28

Upon arrival at the objective Groups B and C would combine to form the relief for Group A which could then retire to LEYTE for replenishment of ammunition.

3. CLOSE AIR SUPPORT UNITS

Of the 18 CVE now temporarily allocated to the 7th Fleet,

it is expected that 9 will be returned for employment in DETACHMENT, after which they will be available for employment in ICEBERG. The remaining 9 will be returned to the control of Pacific Ocean Area Forces about 1 February, in time for use in ICEBERG; these are exclusive of CVE employed as oiler escorts and as ASW units; and are exclusive of transport CVEs.

These 18 CVEs should be disposed approximately as follows:

Screen for advance Fire Support Group	8 CVE
Screen for Amphibious Force mounting in LEYTE	4 CVE
Screen for Amphibious Force mounting in SoPac	4 CVE
Screen for Amphibious Force mounting in MARIANAS	2 CVE

4. MINESWEEPING GROUP

The Minesweeping Group should depart LEYTE or ULITHI in time to reach the objective with the fire support units arriving on D - 6; this group should receive adequate air support from the escort carriers which accompany them and from aircraft of the covering force.

The approach to the objective should be on a northwesterly course leaving KOBA JIMA and KUME SHIMA to the northward then circling to the north, northeast and finally southeast in order to reach a disembarkation area along the western beaches of OKINAWA. The approach courses shown on Annex 3 to Appendix C take advantage of deep unminable waters where possible, through which the fleet can proceed without the necessity of sweeping. Although there is no evidence of mines immediately westward of OKINAWA, the final approach track for a distance of about 20 miles, where depths of less than 500 fathoms are encountered, should be swept on D-6 in order to permit close approach of the fire support group. The area adjacent to selected landing beaches inside the 100 fathom curve should be swept during the period between D-5 and D-1; this area contains about 15 sq. miles.

5. COVERING FORCE

Operations of the Covering Force are described in Appendix B. Battleships and cruisers are expected to be provided with HC ammunition to about 15% capacity; this should be expended against selected targets at the objective. After preliminary air strikes, the operations of the Covering Force will be governed by the activities of enemy naval and air forces, and by requirements for tactical air support at the objective.

PROPOSED ASSEMBLY OF NAVAL FORCES

ANNEX 1 APPENDIX C

ANN

	D-40	D-35	D-30	D-26	D-20	D-15	D-5
GUADALCANAL		11 APA, 3 APH, 1 LSV, 5 LSD, 2 AGC, 50 LST, 20 LSM, 5 APD, 6 AKA — 2 OBB, 1 CB, 1 CA, 5 DD	18 LCI(G), 6 LCI(H), 9 LCI(L), 20 LCT, 3 PC-PCS-SC, 6 YMS — 15 APA, 6 AKA, 9 DD, 1 AGC	2 OBB, 2 CA, 1 CL, 14 DD, 18 LCI(G), 6 LCI(M), 9 LCI(L), 8 PC-PCS-SC, 6 YMS, 20 LSM	4 CVE, 6 DD, 12 DE, 6 DH	4 CVE, 6 DD, 6 DE, 6 DH	
LEYTE			29 APA, 1 LSV, 2 LSD, 12 AKA, 2 AGC, 50 LST, 20 LSM, 6 APD				
NOUMEA							15 APA, 6 AKA, 9 DD, 6 DE, 1 AGC, 6 YMS, 25 LST, 10 LSM

For Troops in Area Reserve
15 APA
6 AKA
10 LST
6 PC-PCS-SC
6 DE
5 LSM

PROPOSED ASSEMBLY OF NAVAL FORCES (Cont'd)   ANNEX 1   APPENDIX C

	D-40	D-35	D-30	D-26	D-20	D-15	D-5
ULITHI							
MARIANAS			15 APA 6 AKA 8 DD 1 AGC 1 LSD 25 LST 10 LSM 5 APD	5 OBB 2 CA 2 CL 18 DD 8 CVE 6 DE	24 DMS 24 AM 6 ATF 2 ATR 1 AKN 4 AN 6 YMS 20 PC-PCS-SC	2 CVE 6 DD 6 DE	For Troops in Area Reserve 15 APA 6 AKA 1 AGC 10 LST 6 PC-PCS-SC 6 DE 5 LSM
ESPIRITU				76 DD			

Units of Covering Force are not included, as this Force will be previously organized and assembled. The Covering Force will contain the following:

8 BB   7 CA
11 CV   7 CL
7 CVL   4 CL(AA)
            76 DD

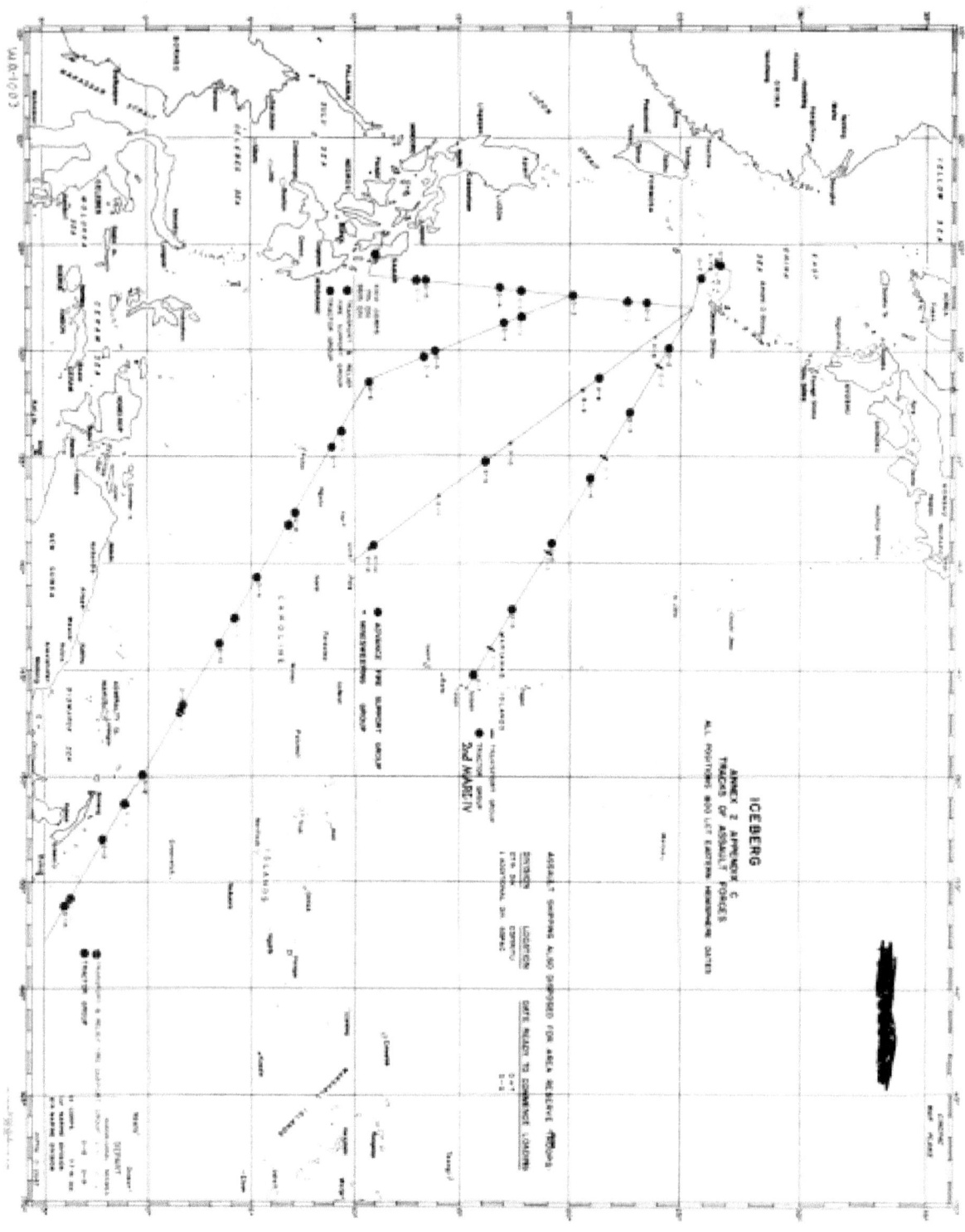

ICEBERG

ANNEX 2 APPENDIX C
TRACKS OF ASSAULT FORCES
ALL POSITIONS 800 LCT EASTERN HEMISPHERE DATES

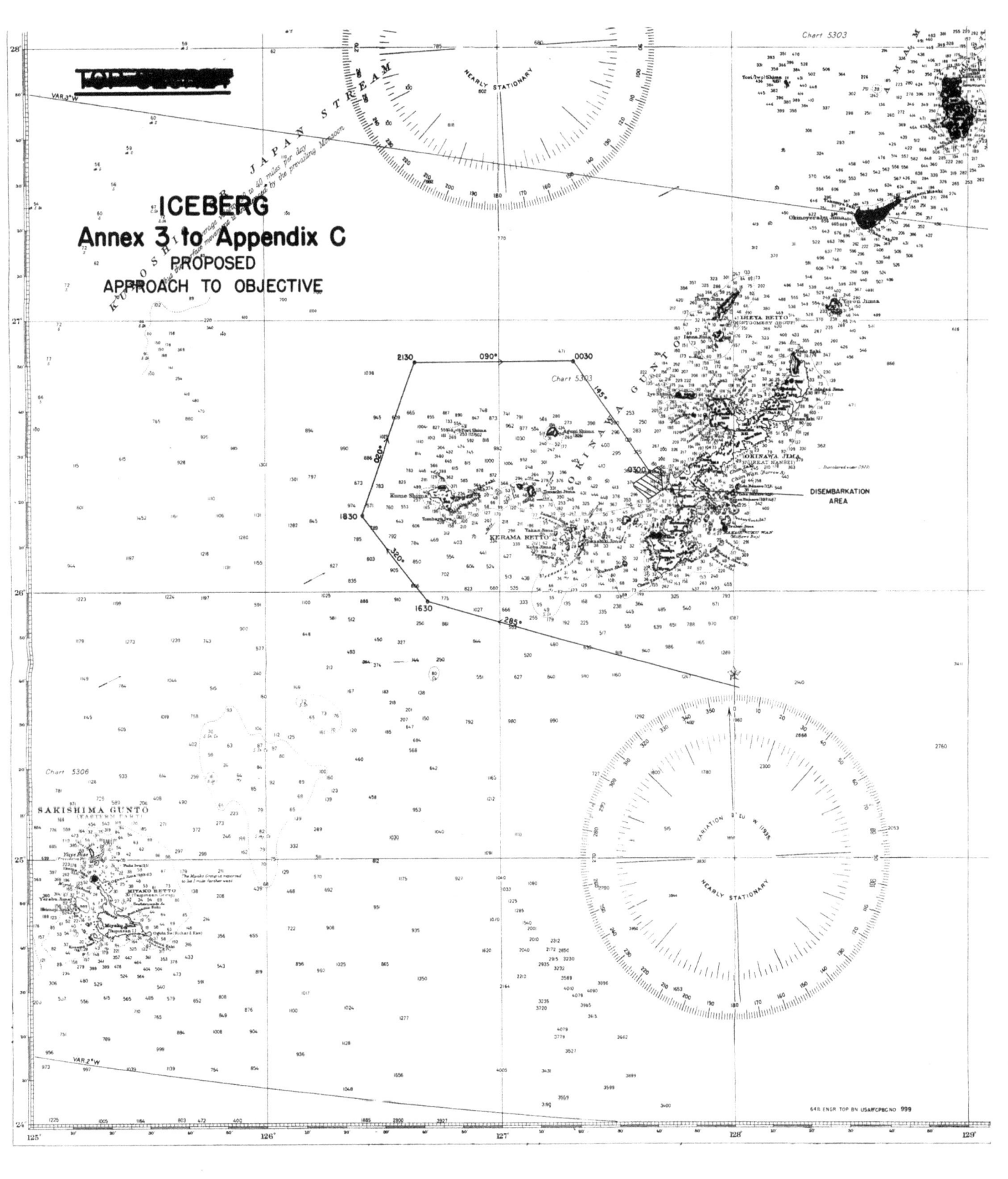

ICEBERG
Annex 3 to Appendix C
PROPOSED
APPROACH TO OBJECTIVE

ICEBERG

Appendix D

Submarine Operations

1. DISCUSSION.

Commencing about February 1, it is expected that shore based aircraft operating from NORTHERN LUZON will effectively close the LUZON STRAIT to enemy shipping; will reduce the flow of shipping to and from the SOUTH CHINA SEA to a fraction of its present volume; and will constrict the area used by this shipping to a relatively narrow belt close to the CHINA coast. Unless cargo is transhipped by land carriers through CHINA, all ships carrying even this reduced cargo must pass through the FORMOSA STRAIT.

Inability to use this shipping from the southern area coupled with an increased demand for imports from North CHINA, will tend to increase greatly the volume of shipping from JAPAN to KOREA, SHANGHAI and other North CHINA ports.

The danger of being bottled up in the SOUTH CHINA SEA Area will probably induce the Japanese to move all important naval combatant units to the EMPIRE either before or immediately after our operation against LUZON. Thus the requirement for our submarines in the southern area should be greatly reduced.

2. TASKS.

The augmented submarine force in the Northern Area should be disposed to perform the following tasks:

(a) Provide life-guard service in the vicinity of OKINAWA from D-30 to D-7; and in designated EMPIRE areas from D-20 to D/20; and in designated areas around FORMOSA and SAKISHIMA GUNTO from D-20 to D/15.

(b) Provide strong submarine patrols south of
OKINAWA JIMA and north of AMAMI O SHIMA in order to
intercept and destroy enemy forces attempting to threaten
our operation or attempting to retire from the area.

(c) Maintain patrols in areas around commercial
terminals in the EMPIRE; in the area north of FORMOSA
STRAIT; and across the shipping lanes from the EMPIRE
to North CHINA ports; in order to inflict maximum attrition
on enemy shipping.

(d) Be prepared to concentrate as required to provide strategic or tactical support of the 5th Fleet.

3.   RESTRICTIONS.

Operating zones and bombing and attack restrictions
will be prescribed in the Current CinCPOA Operating Procedure,
with addenda and zone notices as required.

ICEBERG

APPENDIX E

LOGISTIC MEASURES

Appendix E is based upon the logistical requirements for Phase I only.

ICEBERG

APPENDIX E

LOGISTIC MEASURES

1.   OPERATIONAL REQUIREMENTS

The concept of operations requires:

a. Early establishment of facilities for fleet anchorage with logistic support at NAKAGUSUKU BAY; and eventual development of an advanced fleet base.

b. Rapid construction of airdrome facilities sufficient to support the air program.

c. Expansion of the port of NAHA to support assault and garrison forces, planned developments in the area, and to mount forces for subsequent operations.

d. Installation of service elements to accomplish tasks of development.

2.   FACTS AFFECTING LOGISTICS

a. Approximate Distances From OKINAWA To:

	Nautical Miles	Approx. Sailing time (10 knots) Days
SAN FRANCISCO	6246	26.
PEARL HARBOR	4155	17.3
ENIWETOK	2145	9.
GUAM	1200	5.
ULITHI	1200	5.
PALAU	1200	5.
GUADALCANAL	2860	11.
MANILA	1000	4.
DAVAO	1360	5.7
CANTON	865	3.6
AMOY	535	2.2
FORMOSA (TAKAO)	555	2.3
SHANGHAI	450	1.9
SASEBO	440	1.8
SHIMONOSEKI	485	2.
OSAKA	635	2.6
TOKYO	840	3.5
VLADIVOSTOK	1055	4.4

b. Geography

OKINAWA JIMA, the largest island in the NANSEI SHOTO, lies between 26° 03' and 26° 52' N latitude and between 127° 41' and 128° 20' E longitude, commanding the sea approaches to the China Coast. The island was a key point in the communication between JAPAN and the islands under Japanese Mandate. It is a long narrow island (67 miles long and 3 to 10 miles wide), made up of plateaus and ridges with many bays offering sheltered anchorage. NAKAGUSUKU, the foremost of these, has long been used as a fleet base by the Japanese Navy. The island has a total population of 443,000 mostly concentrated in the southern half. NAHA, the largest city on the island, (66,000) is the capital of the island group.

c. Climate

The climate of the OKINAWA Area is controlled by the monsoonal circulation between the Asiatic Continent and the North Pacific Ocean. From October through March winds blow in a clockwise direction out of the region of high pressure in SIBERIA, and the resulting air flow over these islands is from the north and northeast. During April and May there is a gradual reversal in the direction of air flow, and from June through August the winds over the islands are predominatly south and southeast, a part of the clockwise circulation around the center of high pressure in the North Pacific Ocean. During the transitional months of April, May and September, the direction of air flow usually alternates several times between northeast and south. Fog and dust rarely occur on these islands. The climate is sub-tropical to tropical with mean variation only 17° to 20°. Average daily maximum temperature in summer 85° - 88° with mean daily minimum of 72° - 79°. Air temperature in winter averages between 55° and 65°. Annual precipitation is heavy and by months is somewhat erratic. Frequently a day's downpour will equal the whole monthly average. In general summer months have the greatest precipitation. Winter precipitation, however, occurs over more extended periods than in summer. Average number of days with precipitation (.004 inches or more) are shown in the following table. Figures in parentheses indicate the average inches of rainfall.

	NAHA
January	19(5½)
February	18(4½)

		NAHA
March		18(6)
April		16(5)
May		17(10⁄)
June		16(8)
July		16(7½)
August		19(7½)
September		18(7)
October		16(6½)
November		16(5½)
December		17(4½)

The following table indicates the average number of days with specified cloud cover as of 0600 L.S.T.

		NAHA
	.7 or more	24
January	.4 - .6	2
	.3 or less	5
	.7 or more	22
February	.4 - .6	2
	.3 or less	7
	.7 or more	22
March	.4 - .6	3
	. 3 or less	6
	.7 or more	21
April	.4 - .6	2
	.3 or less	7
	.7 or more	25
May	.4 - .6	3
	.3 or less	3

		NAHA
	.7 or more	24
June	.4 - .6	3
	.3 or less	3
	.7 or more	18
July	.4 - .6	5
	.3 or less	8
	.7 or more	19
August	.4 - .6	5
	.3 or less	7
	.7 or more	19
September	.4 - .6	3
	.3 or less	8
	.7 or more	18
October	.4 - .6	3
	.3 or less	10
	.7 or more	18
November	.4 - .6	4
	.3 or less	8
	.7 or more	22
December	.4 - .6	3
	.3 or less	6

d. Topography

The CHIMA WAN, a bay on the west coast of OKINAWA roughly divides the island in two parts. The northern portion is hilly with elevations up to 1500 feet. The southern half is less rugged and is better adapted for the development of a military base incorporating an anchorage, harbor improvements, flying fields, and other facilities ashore, being mostly of rolling and terraced hill land.

<u>e</u>. Hydrography

The most important feature of OKINAWA'S hydrography is the existence of two large bays on the eastern coast -- NAKAGUSUKU BAY and CHIMU BAY. These waters are extensive in area and offer good depths for anchorage. Large areas of land level enough for base development lie close to these protected waters. The chief difficulty in constructing ship unloading facilities is the width of the coral reefs which fringe the shores.

<u>f</u>. Water Supply

Because of the limestone formation of SOUTHERN OKINAWA, streams and other sources of water near the surface are scarce. Most of the many shallow wells to be found are polluted. It is believed that a sufficient supply of water can be obtained by drilling deep wells in certain areas. However, initially the employment of both distillation and purification units is indicated. NAHA had in 1936 a municipal water system supplying 400,000 gallons per day. It served 23% of the population as well as the wharves. There are 3,676 wells in the city, the water from which is polluted and unpalatable.

<u>g</u>. Survey of Airfield Sites

While complete topographic data is not yet available it is possible to locate existing airfields and tentatively select sites for others. Fields now operative or under construction are the NAHA Field (3 runways), MACHINATO (1 runway), KATENA (1 runway), YONTAN (3 runways), and YONABARU (1 runway). Some of these have well developed dispersal areas with revetments. The small island of IE SHIMA has a field with three (3) runways and evidences of two more underway. Most of the possible sites lie in the coastal flats in the southern portion of OKINAWA but additional runways of fighter length may be feasible in the northern portion.

<u>h</u>. Health and Sanitation

(1) General

There is very little direct information as to health conditions on the target. Due to the climate, water supply, type of sewage disposal and number and type of civilian population on the island, it should be assumed that health conditions will be poor. Mosquitoes are numerous throughout the year.

(2) Civilian Population

There is a low standard of public health and medical facilities on this island. Living conditions are inferior to those in JAPAN. Night soil is used as fertilizer. Rats and disease bearing insects are common. Some locally produced foods are said to be sufficient; however, rice must be imported. Nutritional deficiency diseases are present.

    (3) <u>Diseases</u>

        The following diseases will be of military importance:

            Malaria

            Enteric diseases (diarrheas, dysentery and parasites)

            Scrub typhus

            Dengue

            Filariasis

            Venereal diseases

            Skin diseases

        The following diseases are of potential importance:

            Cholera

            Plague

            Relapsing fever

            Schistosomiasis

            Typhus

            Tuleremia

            Yellow fever

i. <u>Communication Survey</u>

    (1) <u>Telephone, telegraph and cable</u>

        (a) Submarine Cable

            OKINAWA has a submarine cable connection with FORMOSA and JAPAN via other islands of NANSEI SHOTO, and also with YAP. Terminals for these cables are in the vicinity of NAHA and SANAPI.

        (b) Telephone and Telegraph Systems

            NAHA is the center of a telephone and telegraph system connecting principal places on the island. Size and guage of the cables are unknown.

        (c) All plans for communication installations should be prepared on the premise that no enemy equipment or material will be salvageable and that all necessary equipment must be supplied.

(2) Radio

Existing radio installations in OKINAWA Area are as follows:

IZENA SHIMA - one station - 45 miles North of NAHA.

OKINAWA - four stations within 3 miles of NAHA.

KUME SHIMA at GIMA - one station - 47 miles West of NAHA.

ZAMAMI or YAKABI SHIMA - one station - 17 miles West of NAHA.

AGUNI SHIMA - one station 32 miles Northeast of NAHA.

Existing lookout stations are as follows:

HEDO SAKI on Northern tip of OKINAWA.

KUME SHIMA.

CHIYAMU ZAKI on Southern tip of OKINAWA.

A power plant is located near NAHA NAIKO.

A radar tower is reported in vicinity of NAHA.

The southern portion of OKINAWA is apparently suitable for radio transmission and reception to East, South and West.

j. Public Utilities

(1) Electric Light and Power Facilities

The OKINAWA Denki Kaisha (Electric Company) supplies electricity for light and power in both NAHA and SHURI. The generators of this company are run by steam from coal-fired boilers and their capacity in 1938 was 2300 KW. It is believed that there are small generators in the larger villages and towns. No gas installations have been reported.

(2) Water System

The only extensive water piping system on the island was completed at NAHA in 1935. In 1938, it served 3,244 households with 400,000 gallons of water per day over 30 miles of pipe.

(3) Sewerage

NAHA has the only modern sewage system with $3\frac{1}{4}$ miles of pipe.

k. Military Government *See Next Page* —

Discussion will be issued separately at a later date.

l. Transportation

(1) Roads

The rugged terrain features of the Northern half of OKINAWA JIMA have

- 35 -

2.   FACTS AFFECTING LOGISTICS.

    k.   Military Government.

        (1) Characteristics of Inhabitants.

            The population in 1940 was 442,497. This is a population density
of about 1,000 per square mile compared to only 243 per square mile on SAIPAN.
However, since the population is concentrated in the southern portion, the den-
sity in that portion which we expect to develop is far higher. There are two
principal towns, one with a population of 65,700 and a second with 17,500. The
population is more than 20 times that of GUAM while the area is only twice as
great. The natives of this area are not true Japanese. The area was semi-inde-
pendent with political and cultural ties with China until 1879. Since that date
the Japanese have imposed their educational and political system on the natives
with marked success. However, the fact that practically all governmental, educational and commercial posts are filled by Japanese from the main islands and the
fact that mainland Japanese look down upon the natives has led to some degree
of resentment.

            These natives are the same type as those found upon SAIPAN and
TINIAN as the latter emigrated from the OKINAWA area in search of better living
conditions. In OKINAWA the great majority of the people are small scale farmers
and fisherman. The standard of living is lower than on the main islands of
Japan. Generally speaking the people are poorly educated and will be apathetic
both towards our forces of occupation and towards making any effort to aid them-
selves under the occupation. The small element of the population from the main
islands will, if possible, be repatriated by the Japanese before occupation and
those who fall into our hands will be antipathetic and must be placed under
detainment pending screening and probable internment.

        (2) Plans for Administration.

            (a) Law and Order.

                No figures are available on the number of mainland Japanese we
may expect to find. However, to provide for internment of these and of such elements among the natives as may be potentially dangerous, provision must be made
for an internment camp capable of expansion to hold 10,000 people. During the

- 1 -

                                                      ENCLOSURE (A)

assault phase this camp will consist merely of a wire enclosure and emergency shelter constructed of salvaged materials.

(b) Labor

Central pools of laborers will be established under Military Government officers designated as labor supervisors. The allocation of laborers will be on a priority basis and under uniform wage scales established by the Island Commander. Payment of wages due will be centralized under Military Government finance officers and be chargeable to the allotment of funds made available to the service involved.

It is estimated that the Military Government section of the Island Commander's staff will be able to furnish upwards of 30,000 civilian laborers should any such number be required. The rate at which they could be furnished will depend on the rapidity with which civilians come through our lines and the extent to which they have been demoralized by the preliminary assault. Such labor, however, will be very largely unskilled and will require provision of interpreters and supervisory personnel.

(c) Finance.

CNO Top-Secret Serial 0210513 of 9 September advises that the JCS have approved in principle the issuance of supplementary military yen currency for use in troop pay disbursements, military government, and other official purposes. For the OKINAWA area 300,000,000 Yen of this currency will be provided initially. Other yen currency, which is legal tender in the area, will continue in circulation and will be inter-changeable at par with the Supplementary Military Yen. Transaction in any other currency will be prohibited. No exchange rate between the military yen brought in by our forces and U.S. dollars has been established to date. All supplemental military yen will be in the custody of Military Government finance officers. Allotments will be made on request to all military units for troop payments and other expenses.

(d) Industry

Sugar refining on a small scale is the only industry of even minor importance on the island. As in the case of SAIPAN it is expected the mills will be destroyed and the sugar cane fields will be required either for military installations or to produce subsistence crops for the civil population.

- 2 -

There are unimportant iron, coal and sulphur deposits in the North Central section, salt beds and a small quarry in the southern section. The quarry could be worked for building or road-making materials.

The principal agricultural products are sugar cane and sweet potatoes. Sugar cane is the commercial crop and sweet potatoes the major subsistence crop. Small scale stock-raising is widespread and pork constitutes a major item in the native diet. Fishing is important to the native subsistence. It is estimated that the displacement of the population necessitated by the development of military installations on the best agricultural land plus the cessation of fishing, dispersal of livestock and the demoralized condition of the population will make necessary the importation of food for the civil population and that it will be a considerable period before this can be corrected in part by importation of seed and implementation of an agricultural program.

(e) Resources Useful to Us

Aside from labor and a very limited amount of building materials no resources can be expected. An agricultural program and restoration of fishing can contribute towards the support of the civilian population.

ENCLOSURE (A)

precluded the development of even the primitive road net found in most of the Japanese Islands. The developing of a road system sufficient for our military needs would involve considerable equipment and time. Railroad facilities are not known to exist in this area.

The southern half of OKINAWA JIMA has a population upwards of 300,000 people, which would indicate an intricate road net for the area. The only road known to support two lanes of traffic is a short stretch of a few miles connecting NAHA and SHURI. This road is surfaced with stone blocks. It is doubtful if it would support American military traffic. Roads that correspond to arterial highways, appear to be only 12 feet wide and of coral surfacing. Other roads are probably like our country lanes. The use of horse-drawn 30-inch narrow guage railroads is evidence that local roads will not support ordinary traffic requirements.

Until aerial photographic coverage is available to indicate otherwise, it must be assumed that a complete rebuilding of the OKINAWA JIMA road net will be necessary. Such expedients as one-way traffic, separate routes for track-laying type of vehicles and rigid traffic control are indicated.

The study of local materials available for road construction and the nature of the terrain in the southern half of OKINAWA JIMA would indicate that excellent roads can be constructed with modern equipment. Three two-lane all-weather highways, in and out of NAHA, will be required for military purposes including the moving of cargo handled at the port. A like number of similar roads will be required for the movement of cargo, to and from discharge facilities on NAKAGUSUKU WAN.

(2) Railways

A 30-inch guage steam railroad connects NAHA with West Coast communities on the southern half of OKINAWA. It is probable that these railroads have been used for transportation of the heavier military equipment used by the Japanese in the island fortification program. A cross-island branch also connects NAHA with YONABARU on NAKAGUSUKU BAY. To what extent the horse-drawn lines running south from NAHA to ITOMAN and north along the east coast from YONABARU can be adopted to military traffic cannot be determined at this time. Lack of information on the condition of road beds and equipment, and the probability of

destruction as a defense measure makes the use of the railway questionable.

    m. Harbors

        (1) Capacity

            Little is known of the existing cargo handling capabilities either of NAHA Port or facilities on NAKAGUSUKU BAY. It is estimated that the existing waterfront facilities at NAHA will accommodate 50,000 MT per month and with improvement of shore transportation facilities increase to 105,000 MT per month. A moderate dredging program in NAHA Port to improve the channels for shallow draft vessels (LST, LCT, LSM, etc.) should increase the port capabilities by an additional 120,000 MT per month, aggregating a maximum of 225,000 MT per month one way. Present intelligence indicates that facilities in NAKAGUSUKU BAY will have to be new construction.

        (2) Facilities

            Existing facilities at NAHA consists of a 835 foot cement pier and a 475 foot cement pier, with approximately 18 feet of water alongside. The configuration of the harbor entrance precludes ships larger than an LST. It should be noted that the sinking of an LST within the harbor might immobilize the waterfront facilities. Aerial photography may disclose facilities in NAKAGUSUKU BAY of which we are not now aware. Additional facilities for small craft serving the fleet will be required.

        (3) Berths

            Bow and stern moorings to accommodate 10 ships will be required at NAHA. Ample anchorage areas are available at NAKAGUSUKU BAY.

        (4) Development

            Operations in the vicinity of NAHA will be from bow and stern moorings by barge or landing craft to shore facilities. Piers or wharves for liberty ships are not practicable. Prevailing weather conditions make the use of pontoon type piers undesirable.

            In the absence of intelligence to the contrary, it will have to be assumed that beach landings in NAKAGUSUKU BAY will accommodate discharge of cargo until shore facilities can be constructed. Development of 13 Liberty ship berths is desirable and should be constructed if practicable.

3.   TROOP AND TONNAGE REQUIREMENTS

    a.   In setting up the troop lift and tonnage requirements, the following assumptions are made:

(1) Estimated tonnage lift per man

	Org. Equip. Initial Maint. and Const. Material		
	Total Lift	Initial Lift	Later Echelon
Divisional Corps & Army Tactical Troops	5 MT	2	3
All other Troops	10 MT	5	5
Subsequent Maint. Requirements	.8 MT per man per month		

(2) Loading Capacities without Stowage

    AP's - 1500 personnel and 2000 MT

    AK's - 9000 MT

ESTIMATED PERSONNEL LIFT

	1st Month	2nd Month	3rd Month	4th Month	5th Month	6th Month	7th Month	8th Month	9th Month	TOTAL
Div., Corps, & Army Tactical Troops	159,000	43,000								202,000
Other Troops	25,000	27,000	40,000	20,000						112,000
Replacements		3,000	3,000	3,000	1,000	(Omitted from Population)				10,000
TOTAL TROOPS	184,000	73,000	43,000	23,000	1,000					324,000
Assault Shipping Lift	160,000	45,000								205,000
Flight Echelons	1,000	3,000								4,000
Garrison Shipping Lift	23,000	25,000	43,000	23,000	1,000					119,000
AP's Required	15	17	29	15	1	(@ 1500 per AP)				77
POPULATION ESTIMATE										
Balance Forward	-	184,000	254,000	294,000	274,000	224,000	174,000	162,000	-	-
Total Troops from above	184,000	70,000	40,000	20,000						314,000
SUB-TOTAL	184,000	254,000	294,000	314,000	274,000	224,000	174,000	162,000	162,000	152,000
Withdrawals	-	-	-	40,000	50,000	50,000	12,000	(Less Replacements)		
Estimated Population	184,000	254,000	294,000	274,000	224,000	174,000	*162,000	162,000	162,000	(* Used as Basis for supply level)
ESTIMATED DISCHARGE CAPABILITIES IN MT	277,500	375,000	437,000	500,000	500,000	500,000	500,000	500,000	500,000	-

Beach capacities estimated are for garrison type of cargo and are based on very meager information. A new study will be made as soon as aerial photographic interpretations are available. Experience in the MARIANAS indicates that assault type of cargo will exceed these estimates during the assault phase.

- 39 -

ESTIMATE OF TOTAL LIFT OF ORIGINAL EQUIPMENT, INITIAL MAINTENANCE AND CONSTRUCTION MATERIAL

Div., Corps & Army Troops	@ 5 M.T. per man	202,000 x 5 equals	1,010,000
Other Troops	@ 10 M.T. per man	112,000 x 10 equals	1,120,000
		TOTAL	2,130,000

ESTIMATE OF TONNAGE LIFT IN M.T.

	1st Month	2nd Month	3rd Month	4th Month	5th Month	6th Month	7th Month	8th Month	9th Month	TOTALS
Maintenance @ .8 M.T/man	147,000	203,000	235,000	219,000	179,000	139,000	130,000	130,000	130,000	
Build-up Supply Level	-	27,000	36,000	67,000	130,000					260,000
Civil Affairs **	9,000	27,000	18,000	18,000	18,000	18,000	18,000	18,000	18,000	
Div., Corps & Army Troop Totals	320,000	86,000								} 2,130,000
Other Shipping	125,000	200,000	200,000	200,000	180,000	343,000	352,000	124,000		}
TOTAL	601,000	543,000	489,000	504,000	507,000	500,000	500,000	272,000	148,000	
Lifted in Assault Ship	320,000	80,000								400,000
Lifted in Garrison AP	30,000	34,000	58,000	30,000	2,000			(@ 2000 MT)		154,000
Lifted in AK	251,000	429,000	431,000	474,000	505,000	500,000	500,000	272,000	148,000	
AK Required *	28	48	48	54	56	56	56	30	16	
AK Involved (120 day turn around)	28	76	124	178	206	214	222	198	158	

(* Less Assault Shipping to be reused to lift Rear Echelons of Tactical Troops)

** Tentative for estimation purposes only.

4. CONTEMPLATED DEVELOPMENT

PROJECT	CONSTR. TROOPS REQUIRED	M. T. ORGANIZATIONAL AND SPECIAL EQUIP'T	CONSTR. DAYS TO PLACE IN OPER. STATUS	CONSTR. DAYS FOR FINAL COMP.	M. T. CONSTR. MATERIAL
Field #1 4 VMF - 72 1 VMF (N) - 12	1 - NCB - 1115	8959	40 days (Strip + 20% Taxiways & Hardstands)	180 days	17,300
Field #2 4 VMF - 72 1 VMF (N) - 12	1 - NCB - 1115	8959	20 days (Strip + 95% Taxiways & Hardstands)	150 days	17,300
Field #3 4 VMF - 72	1 - NCB - 1115	8959	30 days (Strip completed)	180 days	17,300
Field #4 4 VMF - 72	1 - NCB - 1115	8959	40 days (Strip + 20% Taxiways & Hardstands)	180 days	17,300
Field #5 8 VBH - 96	1 AvEngBn - 804	7140	40 days (Activated for Fighters 3 days after seizure) (Strip + 30% Taxiways & Hardstands) 40 days	180 days	25,000
Field #6 4 VBM - 64	1 AvEngBn - 804	7140	(Activated for Fighters 3 days after seizure) 20 days (Strip + 80% Taxiways & Hardstands)	150 days	17,900

< >
PROJECT	CONSTR. TROOPS REQUIRED	M. T. ORGANIZATIONAL AND SPECIAL EQUIP'T.	CONSTR. DAYS TO PLACE IN OPER. STATUS	CONSTR. DAYS FOR FINAL COMP.	M. T. CONSTR. MATERIAL
Field #7 4 VBM - 64 1 Photo REC - 12 1 Combat Map - 12	1 AvEngBn - 804	7140	(Activated for Fighters 5 days after seizure) 30 days (Strip ≠ 85% Taxiways & Hardstands)	160 days	25,000
Field #8 2 PB(HL) - 24 2 VMTB - 36	1 - NCB - 1115	8959	(Activated for Fighters 5 days after seizure)	150 days	18,000
Field #9	1 - NCB - 1115	8959	40 days (Strip, Taxiways and Hardstands Complete)	180 days	11,600
Navy LION 2 PB (MS) 1 RES SQN.	7 - NCB - 7805	50981	120 days	180 days	109,000
Seaplane Base			50 days	180 days	
Army Storage & Facilities	3 - Engr. Con. Bn. - 2845	16200	-	-	21,600
Harbor and Waterfront Facilities	3 - NCB - 3345	27849	45 days	180 days	42,000
Road Constr.	3 - NCB - 3345	21849	-	180 days	15,000
Misc. Constr. (dumps, Depot, Hq. Hosp. Rehab. Camps, Utilities, Civil Affairs, etc.)	8 - NCB - 8920	58264	-	180 days	100,000
TOTALS	3 AvEngBn - 2412 3 EngBn - 2845 27 - NCB -30,105 35,462 Total Personnel	250317			454,300

NOTE: (1) Measurement tons of construction material for airfields and LION includes BuDocks tonnage in standard components of ACORNS and LIONS, or equivalent for Army and Marine Fields.

(2) Const. Days for operational completion are days required on the site by construction troops with their equipment.

5. EVACUATION PLAN

    a. Casualties and Replacements

        Estimate of Casualties

Dead and Missing	5,000
Local hospitalization	7,000
Requiring evacuation	13,000
Total Casualties	25,000

    b. Surface Evacuation Facilities Required

Casualties will be evacuated by surface vessels from the target to the MARIANAS, supplemented by air evacuation as soon as suitable landing fields are available. Sufficient hospitalization will be provided in GUAM and SAIPAN to stage these patients. Evacuation from the MARIANAS to rear area hospitals in SoPac and OAHU will be by surface and air utilizing regularly established services as far as possible.

Surface shipping required. It is estimated that a total of 10 AH's will be required, to be utilized as follows: 2 AH's for Fleet Support, 2 AH's for evacuation between the MARIANAS and rear areas, 6 AH's for evacuation from target to MARIANAS. Evacuation from target will require the following:

	Patients	
6 AH	9,000	(3 round trips)
3 APH	2,100	(1 trip)
13 APA	1,900	(1 trip)
	13,000	

    c. Air Evacuation

Air evacuation facilities required:

From	To	No. Patients Per Week	Provided by	Service Beginning
Target	GUAM & SAIPAN	500	ComFwdArea	As soon as suitable air fields are established on target.
SAIPAN	OAHU	200	ComGenPOA (ATC)	D ≠ 21
GUAM	OAHU	200	ComAirPac (NATS)	D ≠ 21
GUAM	SOPAC	200	ComGenPOA (ATC)	D ≠ 21

    d. Care of Civilians   *See Next Page —*

Instructions will be issued separately at a later date.

5.   EVACUATION PLAN

    d.   Care of Civilians

         (1) During the Assault Phase. 340,000 out of a total population of
440,000 live in the southern half of the Island. It is practically certain
that they will be cut off from any possibility of escape to the northern section
and that the principal city of 65,700 and the principal town of 17,500 will be
largely or completely destroyed. Based on the estimated number of civilians in
the area, the anticipated advance of our lines and assuming 10% killed, it is
estimated that the number of civilians within our lines during progressive
phases of the assault will be as follows:

         D ≠ 10   26,200

         D ≠ 20   52,680

         D ≠ 30   150,315

         D ≠ 40   306,000

         Shipping restrictions will curtail issues of food and clothing
and the supply of construction materials to the barest minimum consistent with
sustaining life and curbing the spread of disease. Principal dependence must
be put upon captured stocks of food, clothing and salvaged materials and to this
end all units must be indoctrinated with the vital necessity for turning over
all captured stocks and all captured transport for the use of Military Government. Provision must also be made during later phases of the assault for the
salvage, transfer and temporary storage of all such material.

         Food. Subsistence for assault and garrison phases will be cal-
culated on the basis of an 1800 calorie diet which approximate 20 oz. per person
per day. Requirements for the first 30 days are estimated at 2000 tons of which
approximately 600 tons should be loaded in assault shipping.

         Water. It is anticipated that all sources of water will be pol-
luted and that provision must be made for the supply of potable water for civilians. Rigid enforcement of the principle of sterilization by boiling will be
necessary. Water purification and distillation units will be provided on a
basis of providing one quart of potable water per person per day for a total of
240,000 persons.

         Shelter. Shelter provided in the assault phase will of necessity
be limited to that provided for the wounded and sick.

- 1 -

Administration. Twelve (12) Military Government camp units staffed and equipped to administer 2500 civilians each and capable of expansion to 10,000 capacity during the garrison phase will be established. These camp units do not provide shelter other than for wounded.

Clothing. It is to be expected that large numbers of civilians will come into our lines in rags. No clothing is provided in the assault shipping. Clothes, cloth and findings for 60,000 adults and 60,000 children, approximating 225 measurement tons, should be echeloned in by D $\neq$ 30. Stocks of Red Cross clothing now available on the WEST COAST should be utilized for this purpose.

(2) During the Garrison Phase.

(a) Housing and Camps.

The Military Government camp echelons installed in the Assault Phase will be expanded during the garrison phase by utilization of salvage materials. Housing and buildings, other than warehouses, which are still standing or which are capable of restoration will be utilized for billeting of civilians. Civilians will be billeted on other civilians in undamaged areas where practicable. In accordance with the policy enunciated in JCS 1074/1 of 1 November 1944 and CNO Top-Secret despatch 062252 of November, non-interned homeless civilians will be afforded the minimum shelter necessary for the avoidance of disease and unrest. Existing local resources of materials and labor will be exploited to the maximum and the importation of construction materials for civilian housing will be restricted to the amounts necessary to maintain the foregoing standard when local resources are exhausted. Interned civilians will be afforded shelter equivalent to that provided for prisoners of war.

(b) Medical and Hospital Facilities required for Civilians.

It is estimated that 10,000 beds may be necessary for the care of wounded civilians during and by the end of the assault phase. However limitations of shipping and procurement preclude the furnishing of medical facilities in that amount. In order to furnish required minimal humanitarian medical care reconciled with and adjusted to the limitation of shipping and procurement the following approximate type of medical care is outlined.

- 2 -

ASSAULT PHASE

Required Number	Unit	Off.	Men	Total	Meas. Tons	Remarks
15	G6	120	1185	1305	5400	200-bed Tent Hospitals.
25	G10	25	150	175	1250	Dispensaries for out-patient care with 10 beds each.
* 16	N2A	0	224	224	4208	100-man camp) Housing for Medical
* 4	N4A	0	12	12	592	25-man camp) Personnel
* 3	G14	0	0	0	6	Field Dental Units
1	G18	2	4	6	23	Epidemiology
TOTAL		147	1575	1722	11479	

GARRISON PHASE

Required Number	Unit	Off.	Men	Total	Meas. Tons	Remarks
2	G2	0	0	0	6272	600-bed Quonset
6	N5B	0	0	0	1566	Camp buildings to replace N2A about D plus 180
1	G4	16	172	188	1426	200-bed Quonset
1	G18	2	4	6	23	Epidemiology
TOTAL		18	176	194	9287	

* May arrive in later echelons.

6. LOGISTIC SUPPORT FOR THE FLEET

a. General

Fleet units will utilize the harbors of GUAM, SAIPAN, ULITHI and LEYTE for logistic replenishment. Replenishment will be effected by fleet oilers, ammunition ships, supply ships and Naval Supply Depots in GUAM, SAIPAN and LEYTE.

Limited ship repair facilities will be available at GUAM and in ServRon 10 located in ULITHI and MARIANAS. Limited floating repair facilities will be made available at LEYTE by ConServPac.

Floating storage, fuel, provisions and GSK supplies will be provided by ConServPac.

b. Fleet Ammunition

Surface ships supporting this operation will be loaded with full complement of ammunition. Replenishment ammunition will be provided in AE's and AKE's loaded on the WEST COAST and located at LEYTE, ULITHI, MARIANAS or as directed by Fleet Task Force Commander. A reserve of Fleet ammunition will be available at the Naval Magazine, SAIPAN, and Naval Ammunition Depot, GUAM. Details of loadings of AE's and AKE's will be furnished Fleet Task Force Commanders by CinCPOA.

c. Fleet Fuel

Prior to the sortie from ULITHI by the Fast Carrier Task Force on or about 15 February 1945, all ships, all fleet oilers, and all floating fuel storage at ULITHI will be filled to capacity. It is estimated that there will be available at ULITHI, in floating storage, approximately 600,000 barrels of fuel oil.

Fire support groups and assault forces mounting out from ULITHI, MARIANAS, LEYTE, and SoPac as well as fleet oilers and floating storage temporarily assigned to these locations will also be filled to capacity.

Consumption of fuel oil for all surface forces engaged in the operation is estimated at 6,600,000 barrels, covering a period of approximately 30 days from departure from the various mounting points.

Commercial tankers will continue to deliver their cargoes to ULITHI via ENIWETOK, using convoy system between these two bases. Diversions will be effected by CinCPOA as necessary to meet mounting and staging requirements.

Reserve fuel storage of 300,000 barrels will be available at KWAJALEIN, 450,000 barrels at GUAM, and 150,000 barrels at SAIPAN. Approximately 1,000,000 barrels will be available in SoPac forward storage, as well as 500,000 barrels at MANUS. These latter two storages will be available in emergencies only, subject to arrangement with ComSoPac and CinCSoWesPac respectively.

It is estimated that PEARL storage will be not over 5,000,000 barrels as of 1 March 1945. The distance of 3,500 miles to ULITHI involving an average turn around period of approximately 26 days for commercial tankers places this reserve out of reach, as far as sustaining the operation is concerned once it has commenced.

Total estimated fuel required in the Central and South Pacific combined for the month of March covering the period of this operation may be summarized as follows:

ICEBERG Requirements	6,600,000 bbls.
SoPac Requirements	800,000 bbls.
MARSHALL-MARIANA-LEYTE Requirements	800,000 bbls.
PEARL Requirements	800,000 bbls.
TOTAL	9,000,000 bbls.

Fleet oilers are tentatively assigned for distribution during this operation as follows:

*Immediate support basing on ULITHI (Task Force Oilers)	30
Reserve support MARSHALLS-MARIANAS	4
Local support SoPac	2
Maximum under overhaul	6
	42

*Com5thFleet will assign fleet oilers from this group as required for temporary service during the mounting phase of Amphibious Forces in SoPac and at LEYTE. In addition to the reserve oilers assigned to MARSHALLS-MARIANAS support, Com5thFleet will spot oilers in the MARIANAS as required for Amphibious Forces staging through.

d. Potable Water

In addition to the above, the following 3 AO's and 1 AOG are assigned to potable water service:

SEVERN	(AO61)
OCKLAWAHA	(AO84)
PONAGANSET	(AO86)
TOMBIGBEE	(AOG11)

Each of the AO's carry approximately 100,000 barrels of potable water, plus the normal cargo of drummed lubricants and compressed gases of regular fleet oilers. The AOG carries 15,000 barrels of water. These vessels may be replenished at GUAM. Water supply is also available at MANUS and may be available at LEYTE, depending upon completion of water facilities at the latter base.

In the event the PASIG (AW3) and ABATAN (AW4) are completed in time they will be available for potable water service. Each of these vessels will have a distillation capacity of 120,000 gallons per day.

7.   SUPPORT OF LAND BASED FORCES - GENERAL PLAN

 a. Responsibility for Supply

 ComGenPOA, ComGenFMFPac, ComServPac and ComAirPac will be responsible in accordance with existing policies for the initial supply of all units mounted in the Pacific Ocean Areas, and for the resupply of all personnel and organizations to be located on the captured objectives.

 ComSoPac will be responsible for the provision of adequate areas and accommodations for the rehabilitation or staging of units moved to his area, and for the coordination of the logistic support of all elements of all services stationed in or mounted from his area.

 b. Supplies to Accompany Troops

 The following supplies, in general, will be necessary for the initial support of the operation:

 Thirty (30) days of supply of all classes except ammunition.

 Water in drums or in cans sufficient for 2 gal/man/day for five (5) days.

 Five (5) CinCPOA units of fire for all ground force weapons except artillery and AA will mount with 7 U/F.

 Aircraft munitions as follows:

  Fighters   - 20 Missions

Search Bombers   - 5 Missions

Strike Bombers (VBH)   - 10 Missions

Strike Bombers (VMB)   - 12 Missions

c. **Supply Levels to be Established and Maintained at the Objective**

The following levels of supply will be necessary to furnish continuing support and to provide against losses in supplies from various causes:

Classes I, II, and IV (less construction materials)

Minimum level	- 60 days
Operating level	- 30 days

Class III (less Avn)

Minimum level	- 30 days
Operating level	- 30 days

Class III (Avn)

Minimum level	- 30 days
Operating level	- 30 days

Class V Ground Weapons

10 U/F

Class V Aircraft Munitions

Fighters	- 40 Missions
Search Bombers	- 10 Missions
Strike Bombers (VBH)	- 20 Missions
Strike Bombers (VBM)	- 24 Missions

d. **Reserve Supplies**

(1) **SAIPAN**

Class I - 30 days for 200,000 men

Class II and IV (less construction and aviation material) - 30 days supply for 4 Army Divisions (reinforced)

Class III (less Avn) - 30 days supply drummed products for force of 100,000 men.

Class III (Avn) - 1,000,000 gal. AvGas and related lubes in drums.

Class IV - 15 U/F for 1 Army Division

         20 U/F for 1 155mm Gun Bn

         15 U/F for 1 155mm How Bn

5 U/F for 1 Tank Bn (Army)

15 U/F for 1 AAA Bn (Army)

(2) GUAM

Class II and IV (less construction and aviation material) - 30 days supply for 2 Marine Divisions (reinforced)

30 days supply for 50,000 Navy personnel

Class III - 30 days supply drummed products for ground force of 100,000 men.

1,000,000 gal. AvGas and related lubes in drums.

Class V - 15 U/F for 1 Marine Division

20 U/F for 1 155mm Gun Bn (Marine)

15 U/F for 1 155mm How Bn (Marine)

5 U/F for 1 Marine AA Bn

(3) Service Squadron TEN

Service Squadron TEN, located at ULITHI and the MARIANAS will be stocked with the following supplies:

10 days supply in self-propelled ships of Classes I, II, III (less Avn) and IV for -

Army	-	80,000 men
Navy	-	10,000 men
Marine Corps	-	60,000 men

e. Method of Supply

The following method of supply is tentatively established.

(1) Prescribed stocks for this island will be built up to established levels within 150 days.

(2) All units will be mounted with 30 days of all classes of supplies except Class V, and with 5 U/F.

(3) Essential maintenance supplies for 30 days of all classes (except Class III Avn, and Class V) for all elements of the landing and garrison forces scheduled to be at the objective by D $\neq$ 35 will be loaded on the WEST COAST and sailed approximately D - 40 to arrive at ULITHI on D - 5. This shipment will be held at ULITHI for forward movement on call of Commander Expeditionary Troops. This shipment will constitute the first re-supply shipment and should include one

ship fully loaded with drummed AvGas (30,000 drums) and matching lubes.

(4) The second re-supply shipment should be scheduled to arrive at ULITHI by D / 5 for movement forward on call of Commander Expeditionary Troops. This shipment should contain 20 days supply of all Classes (except Class III Avn and Class V) for all elements of the landing and garrison forces scheduled to be at the objective by D / 35. One ship fully loaded with drummed AvGas (30,000 drums) and matching lubes, will be included in the second re-supply shipment.

(5) Subsequent shipment of maintenance supplies of all Classes (except Class III Avn and Class V) for the support of the garrison forces will be loaded and despatched from the WEST COAST to arrive at ULITHI at 10 day intervals beginning with D / 15. These shipments will consist of approximately 15 days maintenance supplies until the prescribed levels are reached. Thereafter, only sufficient supplies will be included to maintain those levels.

(6) ComServPac will arrange for barges and IX tankers loaded as below. These tankers and barges will be available at ULITHI as indicated to be forwarded to objective on call of Commander Expeditionary Troops. If not called for they will be forwarded to objective as indicated.

No. & Type	Capacity	Cargo	Ready Date at ULITHI	ETA Objective
1 - AOG	12,000 bbl.	AvGas	D	D / 20
1 - AOG	12,000 bbl.	Av Gas	D / 10	D / 30
2 - AOG	12,000 bbl.	6000 MoGas 6000 Diesel	D / 15	D / 25
1 - IX Tanker	70,000	AvGas & Lubes 40,000 MoGas	D / 20	D / 35
1 - IX Tanker	70,000	24,000 Diesel	D / 20	D / 35

(7) Initially all fuel will be supplied in drums. Tank farms or other bulk storage will be provided as soon as practicable.

(8) Ammunition for re-supply of the landing forces will be loaded and despatched to ULITHI for shipment forward on call of Commander Expeditionary Troops. Shipments will be loaded and made as follows:

Five (5) LST's with Artillery ammunition to arrive ULITHI by D - 10. Three (3) AK's each with 8 CinCPOA U/F for 2/3 of 1 Army reinforced division and 1/3 of 1 Marine division reinforced to arrive ULITHI by D - 5.

Three (3) AK's similarly loaded to arrive ULITHI by D ≠ 5.

Three (3) AK's similarly loaded to arrive ULITHI by D ≠ 15.

Three (3) AK's similarly loaded to arrive ULITHI by D ≠ 25.

Three (3) AK's similarly loaded to arrive ULITHI by D ≠ 35.

(9) ComFwdAreaContPac will be prepared to make emergency shipments by air of rations, ammunition and medical supplies.

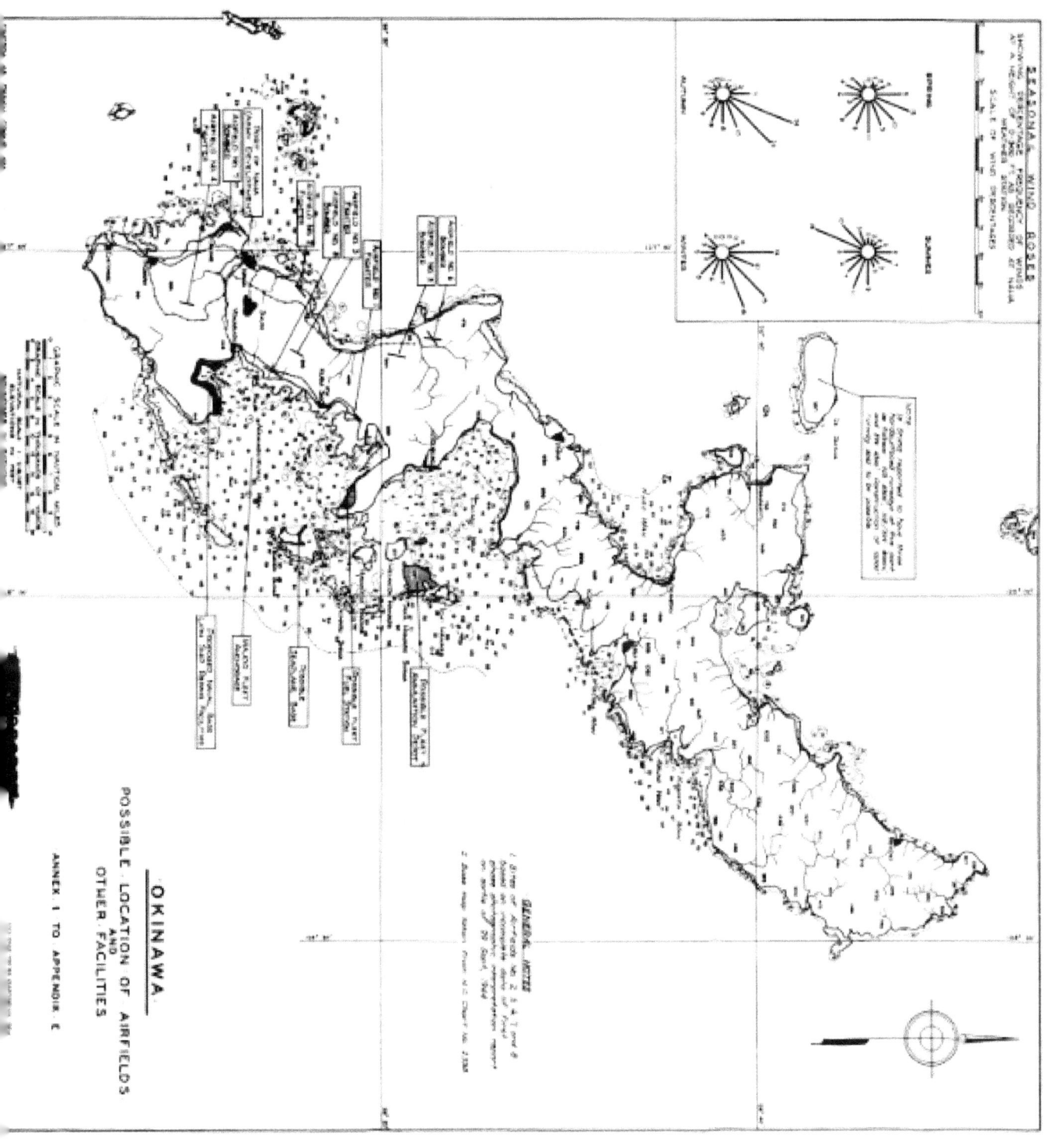

OKINAWA

POSSIBLE LOCATION OF AIRFIELDS
AND
OTHER FACILITIES

ANNEX I TO APPENDIX E

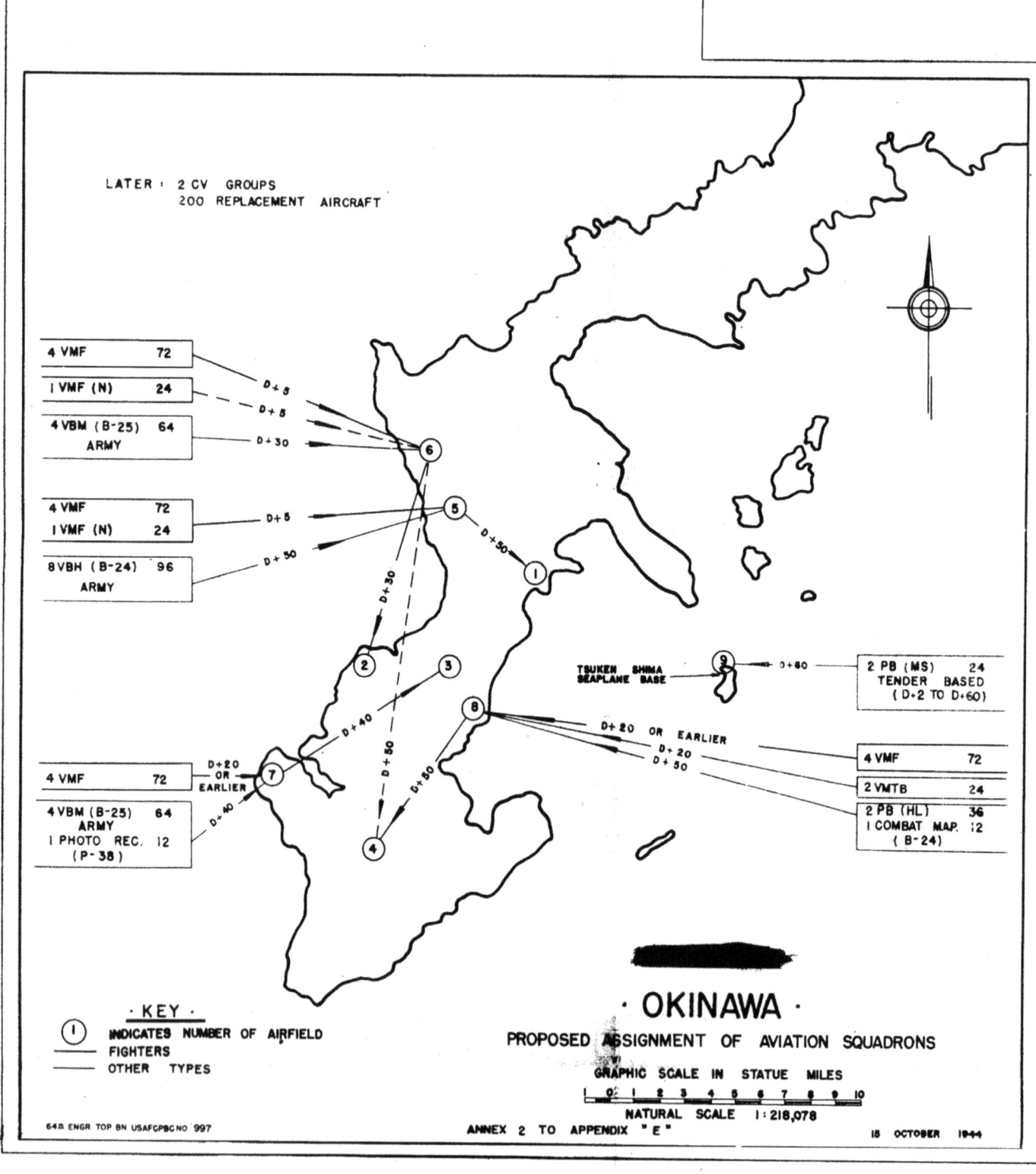

LATER · 2 CV GROUPS
200 REPLACEMENT AIRCRAFT

4 VMF	72
I VMF (N)	24
4 VBM (B-25) ARMY	64

D+5
D+5
D+30

4 VMF	72
I VMF (N)	24
8 VBH (B-24) ARMY	96

D+5
D+50

D+30
D+50

D+40
D+50
D+50

TSUKEN SHIMA
SEAPLANE BASE

D+60

| 2 PB (MS) TENDER BASED (D+2 TO D+60) | 24 |

D+20 OR EARLIER
D+20
D+50

4 VMF	72
2 VMTB	24
2 PB (HL)	36
I COMBAT MAP. (B-24)	12

D+20
OR
EARLIER

4 VMF	72
4 VBM (B-25) ARMY	64
I PHOTO REC. (P-38)	12

D+40

· KEY ·

① INDICATES NUMBER OF AIRFIELD
——— FIGHTERS
——— OTHER TYPES

· OKINAWA ·

PROPOSED ASSIGNMENT OF AVIATION SQUADRONS

GRAPHIC SCALE IN STATUE MILES

0 1 2 3 4 5 6 7 8 9 10

NATURAL SCALE 1:218,078

64ᵗᴴ ENGR TOP BN USAFCPBC NO 997

ANNEX 2 TO APPENDIX " E "

15 OCTOBER 1944

APP

ICEBERG

APPENDIX F

TROOP LIST

S U M M A R Y   O F   P E R S O N N E L

ASSAULT FORCE

(a) Total		238,009
(b) To be used in Garrison Force		82,944
(c) To be withdrawn		155,065

GARRISON FORCES

(a) To be moved to area		77,736
(b) To be provided by Assault Force		82,944
(c) Total		160,680

THIS TENTATIVE LIST OF ASSAULT AND SUPPORTING SERVICE TROOPS
IS DEEMED THE MINIMUM FOR ACCOMPLISHMENT OF PHASE I OF THIS
OPERATION ONLY. THEIR AVAILABILITY HAS NOT BEEN DETERMINED.

ICEBERG

ASSAULT FORCE

Unit	T/O	FIELD ARMY — Army No.	Strength	Navy No.	Strength	Marine No.	Strength	ARMY CORPS T/O	Army No.	Strength	AMPHIBIOUS CORPS T/O	Marine No.	Strength
Headquarters, Field Army	-	(1)	1358										
Headquarters, Corps	-	1	560					100-1	(1)	180			
Headquarters, Company								100-2	1	105			
Hqs & Hqs Dets Sps Troops, Type "C"								200-35-C	1	46	F-850	(1)	1217
Hq and Service Bn.													
Hq & Hq Det Sps Troops, Type "D"	200-35-D	1	66										
Divisions (not reinforced)						113			(5)	71000		(3)	52200
										(includes 2 in' area reserve)			
TOTAL			1984		54		113			71331			53417
AVIATION													
VMF- MAG	D-101					4	3468						
VMF (N) Sqdns	D-108					2	798						
VMTB	D-103					2	680						
F-5 Sqdn (Photo Recon, P-38)	1-757	1	342										
VBM Groups (B-25)	1-112 & 1-127	2	3206										
PB(MS) Sqdns				2	410								
TOTAL			3548		410		4946						
AAA UNITS													
Hq & Hq Btry AA Brig (Opn. Det.)	1-022	1	44										
Hq & Hq Btry AA Group	44-10-1	3	207										
AA Bn Gun Mobile	44-12	2	1486										
AA Bn Gun (SM)	44-15	3	1935										

ICEBERG

ASSAULT FORCE

	T/O	Army No.	Army Strength	Navy No.	Navy Strength	T/O	Marine No.	Marine Strength	T/O	Army No.	Army Strength	T/O	Marine No.	Marine Strength
		FIELD ARMY							**ARMY CORPS**			**AMPHIBIOUS CORPS**		
AAA S/L Bn (SM)	44-135	2	1694											
AAA Bn AW Mob	44-25	1	817											
AAA Bn AW SP	44-75	1	709											
AAA Bn AW (SM)	44-125	3	2289											
AAA Bn - Marine												E-175	4	5040
TOTAL			9181											5040

NOTE: Arrival of AAA units except those required for the assault to be integrated to conform with construction of airfields.

ARTILLERY

	T/O	Army No.	Army Strength	T/O	Army No.	Army Strength	T/O	Marine No.	Marine Strength
Hq & Hq Btry Corps Arty	6-12	1	99	6-50-1	1	112	E-149	1	117
Hq & Hq Btry FA Group				6-12	2	198			
155mm How Bn				6-335	3	1617	E-135	3	1950
155mm Gun Bn				6-357	3	1686	E-185	3	2178
Observation Bn (FA)	6-359	2	1178	6-75	1	505			
8 inch or 240mm How Bn									
TOTAL			1277			4118			4245

TANK DESTROYER

	T/O	Army No.	Army Strength
TD Bns	18-25	1	671

TANKS

	T/O	Army No.	Army Strength	T/O	Marine No.	Marine Strength
Hq & Hq Tank Group	17-22	1	101			
Tank Bns Medium	17-45	4	2916	F-1020	1	869
LVT (Tank) Bns	17-115	3	2331			
TOTAL			5348			869

(one medium tank Bn. incl. orgn. in each Marine Division)

- 53 -

ICEBERG
ASSAULT FORCE

	FIELD ARMY Army			Navy		Marine			ARMY CORPS Army			AMPHIBIOUS CORPS Marine		
	T/O	No.	Strength	No.	Strength	T/O	No.	Strength	T/O	No.	Strength	T/O	No.	Strength
MISC. TROOPS														
Army M P Bn	19-35	2	1112											
Liaison Sqdn (Air)	1-977	1	140											
Field Depot (reinforced)												-	1	2500
Amphib Recon Bn												E-335	1	303
TOTAL			1252											2803
CHEMICAL														
Maint Det	-	1	41											
Depot Co	3-67	1	184											
Chemical Bn Motorized	3-25	1	622											
TOTAL			847											
SIGNAL														
Sig Const Bn	11-25	1	595											
Sig Repair Co	11-127	1	188											
Sig Radio Intelligence Co	11-77	1	259											
Signal Service Bn	-	1	829											
Sig Bn (Corps)									11-5	1	790			
Photo Co	11-37	1	148											
Sig Oper Bn	11-95	1	662											
JASCO	-	3	1131	6	844	-	3	1131						
Sig Serv Bn (Sonic & Deception)	-	1	574											
TOTAL			4386		844			1131			790			793
MEDICAL														
Med Bns	8-15	2	930						11-5	1	465		1	374
TOTAL			930								790			793

ICEBERG

		ASSAULT FORCE								ARMY CORPS			AMPHIBIOUS CORPS		
		FIELD ARMY					Marine			Army			Marine		
	T/O	Army No.	Strength	Navy No.	Strength	T/O	No.	Strength	T/O	No.	Strength	T/O	No.	Strength	
Amb. Co Mtzd Sep	8-317	1	93												
Evac Hosp (400 beds)	-	4	908												
Evac Hosp (600 beds)				1	232								1	232	
Med Lab															
Med Depot Co	8-611	1	58												
Malaria Survey Units	8-661	1	178												
Malaria Control Units															
Epidemiological and Malaria Team G-19															
Surgical Teams	-	10	60	1	102	-			-	3	36				
						-			-	3	36				
TOTAL			2227		334			540						606	

FINANCE

Finance Disbursing Sections	14-500	2	54												

ORDNANCE

Gp Hq & Hq Det	9-12	1	53												
Bn Hq & Hq Det	9-76	8	200												
Bcmb Disposal Sqds	9-179	6	42												
Heavy Maint Co (FA)	9-9	3	594												
Heavy Maint Tk Co	9-37	2	420												
Depot Co	9-57	3	558												
Maint Co AA	9-217	2	326												
Med Auto Maint Co	9-127	3	360												
Hvy Auto Maint Co	9-327	2	422												
Ammo Co	9-17	6	1116												
MM Co	9-9	6	1014												
Evac Co	9-187	1	185												
TOTAL			5290												

Ordnance units in Marine Field Depot

- 55 -

ASSAULT FORCE

		FIELD ARMY								ARMY CORPS			AMPHIBIOUS CORPS		
		Army			Navy			Marine		Army			Marine		
	T/O	No.	Strength	T/O	No.	Strength	T/O	No.	Strength	T/O	No.	Strength	T/O	No.	Strength
AVIATION SERVICE UNITS															
Service Groups (Special)	Est	2	1400												
Hq & Serv SQ (MG)															
AW Sqdns (lt)															
AACS Det	1-447	1	110	D-115, D-116, E-691				4	2600						
Base Hq & Air Base Sqdns	1-422	1	370					4	920						
Aviation Sqdns	1-999	1	253												
M P Co (Aviation)	19-217	1	104												
TOTAL			2237						3520						
ENGINEER															
Engr Hq Corps										5-100-1	1	7			
Engr Hq Army	5-100-1	1	72								1	85			
Hq & Hq Co Engr Comb Gp	5-16	2	170												
Engr Combat Bn	5-15	3	1992							(3 per Corps) (3 per each of 3 Divs)	12	7968			
Engr Lt Pontoon Co	5-87	2	406												
Engr Treadway Bridge Co	5-627	2	288												
Engr Water Supply Co	5-67	1	141												
Engr Maint Co	5-157	1	200												
Engr Topo Bn Army	5-55	1	467												
Engr Dump Truck Co	5-88	3	342												
Engr Lt Equip Co	5-367	2	246												
Naval Const Bn	P-1 Comp													3	3348*
Mar Engr Sep Bn													(one per Mar Div (Navy)) E-285	2	2012
Engr Depot Co	5-47	1	218												
TOTAL			4542									806G			2012

ICEBERG

ASSAULT FORCE

		FIELD ARMY						ARMY CORPS		AMPHIBIOUS CORPS		
	T/O	Army No.	Strength	Navy No.	Strength	T/O	Marine No.	Strength	T/O Army No. Strength	T/O	Marine No.	Strength
QUARTERMASTER												
Gas Supply Co	10-77	2	256									
Serv Bns	10-67	5	4275									
Truck Bns	10-55	3	1461									
Sterilization Cos	10-177	3	477									
Car Cos	10-87	1	135									
Depot Supply Cos	10-227	4	776									
Graves Reg Co	10-297	2	260									
Salvage Collection Cos	10-187	2	418							Depot		
Bakery Co	10-147	3	504									
Hq & Hq Co QM Base Depot	10-520-1	1	154									
Hq & Hq Det QM Gp	10-22	1	32									
Hq & Hq Det QM Bn	10-56	3	51									
Railhead Co	10-197	4	708									
TOTAL			9507									
TRANSPORTATION												
Port Cos	55-117	6	1380	4	100?		5	920				
Base Ccs	F-1			1	109?							
CB Special									Included in			
Amphibious Truck Cos	55-37	11	2112			E-705			Marine Field			
LVT (C) Bn		10	4970			E-50	5	2485				
MT Bn												
TOTAL			8462		2098			3405		F-715	1	619
ADJUTANT GENERAL												
Base P O	12-601	1	98									
Hq & Hq Det Rep Bn	20-46	1	24									

ICEBERG

ASSAULT FORCE

		FIELD ARMY							ARMY CORPS			AMPHIBIOUS CORPS		
	T/O	Army No.	Strength	T/O	Navy No.	Strength	T/O	Marine No.	Strength	T/O	Army No.	Strength	T/O	Marine No.	Strength
Replacement Co	20-47	6	210												
TOTAL			332		3	240									
GARRISON BEACH PARTY															
MILITARY GOVERNMENT**															
M P Bn	19-55	1	678		1 (incl. in Engr Troops)										
Const Bn	P-1														
Misc. Personnel	—		500												
TOTAL			1178												
GRAND TOTAL			62323			7328*			13984			84839			69535

GRAND AGGREGATE TOTAL (ARMY, NAVY, MARINE) - 238,009

NOTES:
* Includes 3348 Navy C.B. personnel listed in Marine Amphibious Corps Column.
** Tentative for estimation purposes only.

ICEBERG

	T/O	TOTAL All Services		GARRISON FORCE FROM ASSAULT FORCES Army		Navy		Marine		ADDITIONAL Army		Navy		Marine	
		No.	Strength	No.	Strength	No.	Strength	No.	Strength	No.	Strength	No.	Strength	No.	Strength
ISCOM AND STAFF															
Hq & Hq Bn		1	700							1	7CO				
NAVAL BASE COMDR															
Staff, NOB		1	25C									1	250		
SHORE BASED AIRFORCE COMDR STAFF															
Hq & Hq Sqdn RS	1-800-15	1	256							1	256				
BOMBER COMMAND HEADQUARTERS		1	251							1	251				
MAW HQ		1	334											1	334
HQ & HQ CO SERVICE COMMAND		1	335							1	335				
CORPS HQ & HQ CO AND SPECIAL TROOPS	100-102 200-35-C	1	331		331										
TOTAL			2457	331	331						1542		250:		334
DIVISIONS - Inf.		2	284CO	2	284CO										
AVIATION															
VMF - MAG	D-101	4	3468											4	3468

ICEBERG

	T/O	GARRISON FORCE FROM ASSAULT FORCES — All Services		Army		Navy		Marine		ADDITIONAL — Army		Navy		Marine	
		No.	Strength	No.	Strength	No.	Strength	No.	Strength	No.	Strength	No.	Strength	No.	Strength
AVIATION (Continued)															
VMF(N) Sqdns	D-100	2	798					2	798						
VMTB Sqdns	D-103	2	680					2	680						
PB(HL) Sqdns		2	410									2	410		
Photo Sq (incl Interp Sq)		1	500									1	500		
F-5 Sqdns (Photo-Recon P-38)	1-757	1	342	1	342										
VBM Groups (B-25)	1-112 & 1-127	2	3206	2	3206										
VBH Groups (B-24)	1-112 & 1-117	2	3510							2	3510				
PB(MS) Sqdns		2	410			2	410								
TOTAL		13324		3548		410		4946		3510		910			
AAA UNITS															
Hq & Hq Btry AA Brig	44-10-1	1	75	1	75										
Hq & Hq Btry AA Gp	44-12	3	207	3	207										
AAA Bn Gun Mobile	44-15	2	1486	2	1486										
AAA Bn Gun (Sm)	44-115	3	1935	3	1935										
AAA S/L Bn (Sm)	44-135	2	1694	2	1694										
AAA Bn AW Mobile	44-25	1	817	1	817										
AA Bns Marine	3-175	4	5040					4	5040						
AAA Bn AW Sp	44-75	1	709	1	709										
AAA Bn AW (Sm)	44-125	3	2289	3	2289										
TOTAL		14252		9212				5040							
ARTILLERY															
Hq & Hq Btry (FA) Gp	6-12	1	99	1	99										

	T/O	All Services		Army		Navy		Marine		Army		Navy		Marine	
		No.	Strength	No.	Strength	No.	Strength	No.	Strength	No.	Strength	No.	Strength	No.	Strength
		TOTAL		FROM ASSAULT FORCES				GARRISON FORCE		ADDITIONAL					
ARTILLERY (Continued)															
1 Hq & Hq Btry CA Gp	4-152	1	75							1	75				
155mm Gun (CA) (Sm) Bn	4-155	3	1614							3	1614 (D/45)				
155mm How Bn	6-335	3	1617	3	1617										
155mm Gun Bn	6-357	3	1686	3	1686										
Observation Bn	6-75	1	505	1	505										
TOTAL			5596		3907						1689				
MISCELLANEOUS TROOPS															
T D Bn	18-25	1	671	1	671										
Tank Bn (Medium)	17-45	1	729	1	729										
M P Bn (Army)	19-35	1	556	1	556										
TOTAL			1956		1956										
CHEMICAL WARFARE															
Depot Co	3-67	1	184	1	184										
Maint Det		1	41	1	41										
TOTAL			225		225										
SIGNAL															
Port Sig. Serv Co	11-327	1	165							1	165				
Sig Serv Organization		1	550	1	550										
Sig Const Cos Hvy	11-27	2	504							2	504				

		TOTAL		GARRISON FORCE FROM ASSAULT FORCES						ADDITIONAL					
		All Services		Army		Navy		Marine		Army		Navy		Marine	
	T/O	No.	Strength	No.	Strength	No.	Strength	No.	Strength	No.	Strength	No.	Strength	No.	Strength
SIGNAL (Continued)															
Sig Constr Bn	11-25	1	456	1	456										
Sig Repair Co	11-127	1	188	1	188										
Sig Depot Co	11-167	1	188							1	188				
Sig Radio Intelligence Co	11-77	1	259	1	259										
TOTAL			2310		1453						857				
MEDICAL															
Special Hosp #3 (aug)		1	355									1	355		
Special Hosp #4 (aug)		1	355									1	355		
Special Hosp #6 (aug)		1	157									1	157		
Special Hosp #7 (aug)		1	157									1	157		
Special Hosp #8 (aug)		1	157									1	157		
G-10 Dispensary		7	42									7	42		
G-18 Epidemiological Unit		4	32									4	32		
Optical Unit, Mobile		1	2									1	2		
Fleet Hospital #106 (1000 bed)		1	130									1	130		
Fleet Hospital #112 (1000 bed)		1	287									1	287		
Base Hospital (1000 bed)		1	328									1	328		
Fleet Hospital #4 (1000 bed)		1										1			
Fleet Hospital #116 (1500 bed)		1	891									1	891		
Optical Unit Base		1	2									1	2		
Med. Storehouse #2		1	55									1	55		
Fleet Dental Clinic		1	24									1	24		
General Hospital (1000 bed)	8-550	2	1180							2	1180				
Station Hospital (500 bed)	8-560	2	702							2	702				

ICEBERG

	T/O	TOTAL All Services		GARRISON FORCE FROM ASSAULT FORCES Army		Navy		Marine		ADDITIONAL Army		Navy		Marine	
		No.	Strength	No.	Strength	No.	Strength	No.	Strength	No.	Strength	No.	Strength	No.	Strength
MEDICAL (Continued)															
Station Hospital (250 bed)	8-560	1	192							1	192				
Station Hospital (150 bed)	8-560	2	294							2	244				
Station Hospital (100 bed)	8-560	2	160							2	160				
Sanitary Cos	8-117	3	351							3	351				
Med Maint Team Type #2		1	9							1	9				
Veterinary Det (food insp)		1	5							1	5				
Dental Prosthetic Team		1	4							1	4				
Amb Co Motorized Sep	8-317	1	93	1	93										
Med Lab	8-611	1	58	1	58										
Med Depot Co	8-661	1	178	1	178										
Malaria Survey Unit		5	65	3	39					2	26				
Malaria Control Unit		5	60	3	36					2	24				
Epidemiological & Malaria Control Component G-19	G-19	1	102			1	102								
TOTAL			6377		404		102				2897		2974		
FINANCE															
Finance & Disbursing Det		1	27	1	27										
TOTAL			27		27										
ORDNANCE															
Ord Gp Hq & Hq Det	9-12	1	53	1	53										
Ord Bn Hq & Hq Det	9-76	3	75	3	75										
M Maint Co	9-217	2	326	2	326										

GARRISON FORCE

	T/O	TOTAL All Services No.	Strength	FROM ASSAULT FORCES Army No.	Strength	Navy No.	Strength	Marine No.	Strength	ADDITIONAL Army No.	Strength	Navy No.	Strength	Marine No.	Strength
ORDNANCE (Continued)															
Med Maint Co	9-9	4	676	4	676										
Ammo Cos	9-17	3	558	3	558										
Ord Auto Maint Co (Hvy)	9-327	1	211	1	211										
Hvy Maint Co. (FA)	9-9	1	198	1	198										
Ord Depot Co	9-57	2	372	2	372										
Bomb Disp Sqds	9-179	3	21	3	21										
Ord Med Auto Maint Co	9-127	2	240	2	240										
Hq Co Ord Base Gp	9-312	1	41							1	41				
Ord Base Auto Maint Bn	9-316	1	449							1	449				
Ord Base Arm Maint Bn	9-315	1	726							1	726				
Ord Tire Repair Co	9-347	1	145							1	145				
TOTAL			4091		2730						1361				
AVIATION SERVICE UNITS															
Service Groups Special	D-115, D-116	4	2800	2	1400					2	1400				
Hq & Serv Sqdns (MAG)	E-691	4	2600					4	2600						
AW Sqdns (M)		4	920					4	920						
ACORNS (less CBs)		2	1000									2	1000		
CASUs		1	420									1	420		
PATSU		1	316									1	316		
Airways Station (CT &RR)	1-447	1	152	1	110					42					
CBMU	P-5	6	1662									6	1662		
Base Hq & Adv Base Sqdns	1-422	3	370	3	370										
Aviation Sqdns	1-999	3	759	3	759										
M P Co (Aviation)	19-217	1	104	1	104										

| | | TOTAL | | GARRISON FORCE FROM ASSAULT FORCES | | | | | | ADDITIONAL | | | | | |
| | | All Services | | Army | | Navy | | Marine | | Army | | Navy | | Marine | |
	T/O	No.	Strength	No.	Strength	No.	Strength	No.	Strength	No.	Strength	No.	Strength	No.	Strength
AVIATION SERVICE UNITS (Continued)															
Signal Co. (Aviation)	11-217	3	543							3	543				
Det Weather Sqdn		1	75							1	75				
TOTAL			11721		2743				3520		2060		3398		
ENGINEER															
Base Engr Hq	5-592	1	72							1	72				
Hq & Hq Co Engr Const Gp	5-72	3	255	3	255										
Engr Const Bn	5-75	3	2703							3	2703				
Engr Petroleum Dist Co	5-327	1	228							1	228				
Engr Dump Truck Co	5-88	8	912	3	342					5	570				
Engr Base Equip Co	5-377	1	184							1	184				
Engr Hvy Shop Co	5-357	1	178							1	178				
Engr Maint Co	5-157	2	400	1	200					1	200				
Hq & Hq Co Base Depot Gp	5-592	1	75							1	75				
Avn Engr Bn	5-415	3	2421							3	2421				
Engr Parts S Plat	5-567	1	59							1	59				
Engr Firefighting Plat	5-502	5	145							5	145				
Engr Serv Organization (EC)	5-500	5	290							5	290				
S/L Maint. Team	5-500	3	9							3	9				
Gas Generating Det	5-500	2	46							2	46				
Engr Base Depot Co	5-267	1	160							1	160				
Naval Const Bn (Avn)	P-1	5	5580									5	5580		
Naval Const Bn (LION)	P-1	7	7812									7	7812		
Naval Const Bn (Seaplane Base)	F-1	1	1116									1	1116		

	T/O	All Services		FROM ASSAULT FORCES						ADDITIONAL					
				Army		Navy		Marine		Army		Navy		Marine	
		No.	Strength	No.	Strength	No.	Strength	No.	Strength	No.	Strength	No.	Strength	No.	Strength
ENGINEER (continued)															
Naval Const Bn (Harbor Const)	P-1	3	3348									3	3348		
Naval Const Bn (Gen Const)	P-1	6	6696			3	3348					3	3348		
Naval CB Brigade Hq		2	156									2	156		
Naval CB Regt Hq		6	402									6	402		
Naval ABC Depot	P-1	1	1116									1	1116		
Engr Water Supply Co	5-67	2	282	1	141					1	141				
Engr Light Equip Co	5-367	2	245	2	246										
TOTAL			34891		1184		3348				7481		22878		
QUARTERMASTER															
Gas Supply Co	10-77	1	128	1	128										
Truck Bn	10-55	1	487							1	487				
Sterilization Cos	10-177	2	318	2	318										
Laundry Cos	10-167	2	546							2	546				
Salvage Repair Co	10-237	2	402							2	402				
Depot Supply Co	10-227	2	388	2	388										
QM Service Cos	10-67	6	1314	6	1314										
Graves Reg Plat	10-297	2	65	2	65										
Salvage Collection Co	10-187	1	209	1	209										
Bakery Cos	10-147	3	504	3	504										
Hq & Hq Det QM Base Depot	10-520-1	1	154	1	154										
Base Depot Co (Supply & sales)	10-387	1	130							1	130				
Hq & Hq Det QM Bn	10-56	2	34	2	34										
TOTAL			4679		3114						1565				

- 66 -

ICEBERG

		TOTAL		GARRISON FORCE FROM ASSAULT FORCES						ADDITIONAL					
		All Services		Army		Navy		Marine		Army		Navy		Marine	
	T/O	No.	Strength	No.	Strength	No.	Strength	No.	Strength	No.	Strength	No.	Strength	No.	Strength
TRANSPORTATION															
Hq & Hq Co Major Port	55-110	1	526							1	528				
Port Cos	55-117	8	1840							2	460				
CBs (Special)	P-1	2	2196	6	1380							1	1098		
Base Cos		20	50C0			1	1098					16	4000		
CB Rgt Hq		1	67									1	67		
Pontoon Oper Bns		2	2436			4	1C00					2	2436		
Truck Cos (N)		4	460									4	460		
TOTAL			12527		1380		2090				988		8061		
ADJUTANT GENERAL															
Base Post Office	12-601	1	98	1	98										
Base Censorship Det	Est	1	136							1	136				
Hq & Hq Det Rep Bn	20-46	1	24	1	24										
Replacement Cos	20-47	6	210	6	210										
TOTAL			468		332						136				
NAVAL BASE UNITS															
Garrison Beach Party		3	240			3	240								
*LION		1	7031									1	7C31		
Naval Supply Depot		incl. in LION pers.										incl. in LION pers.			
*PT Operating Base		1	217									1	217		
*Standard Landing Craft Units		2	2960									2	2960		

*For details see Annex I to Appendix F

NAVAL BASE UNITS (continued)

	T/O	TOTAL All Services		GARRISON FORCE — FROM ASSAULT FORCES Army		Navy		Marine		ADDITIONAL Army		Navy		Marine	
		No.	Strength	No.	Strength	No.	Strength	No.	Strength	No.	Strength	No.	Strength	No.	Strength
*Rec. Station (2000 men)		1	199									1	199		
*Communication Units		1	1161									1	1161		
Fort Cargo and Trans Unit		1	200									1	200		
Fleet Canteen		2	50									2	50		
Officers Club		2	40									2	40		
Naval Ammunition Depot		incl. in LION pers.										incl. in LION pers.			
Aviation Supply Depot		1	400									1	400		
TOTAL			12498				240						12258		

MILITARY GOVERNMENT **

	T/O	All Services No.	Strength	Army No.	Strength	Navy No.	Strength	Marine No.	Strength	Add. Army No.	Strength	Navy No.	Strength	Marine No.	Strength
Central Administration	-19-55	2	1356	1	678			1			678		45		
Public Safety (MP Bns)	2		45								80				
Finance and Supply			80								55				
Economics			55								32				
Law and Courts			32								25				
Property Custodian & Claims			25												
Engineering Public Serv (C Bn) P-1	P-1		1116			1	1116	***			130				
Public Welfare			130								230				
Intelligence, Interpretation Public Relations			230								65				
Labor			65								55				
Transportation			55												

*For details see Annex I to Appendix F
**Tentative for estimation purposes only
***500 Army personnel included in assault force

ICEBERG

GARRISON FORCE

MILITARY GOVERNMENT (Continued)

	T/O	TOTAL All Services		FROM ASSAULT FORCES Army		Navy		Marine		ADDITIONAL Army		Navy		Marine	
		No.	Strength	No.	Strength	No.	Strength	No.	Strength	No.	Strength	No.	Strength	No.	Strength
Camp (250 men) N1A	8	8	176									8	176		
Camp (100 men) N2A	4	4	44									4	44		
Hospital (600 bed) G-2	4	4	1400									4	1400		
Dispensary G-9	8	8	40									8	40		
Camp N5C	8	8	-									8	-		
Dispensary, Dental, G-12	16	16	32									16	32		
TOTAL		4881		1178		1116		13506		895		1692		334	
GRAND TOTAL		160680		62124		7314		13506		24981		52421			
including (a) from Assault		82944													
(b) Additional Units		77736													

ICEBERG

ANNEX I

TO

APPENDIX F

LION

	Unit	No. of Units	Personnel
A-1	Administration	1	175
A-5	Intelligence	1	9
A-7	Shore Patrol	3	69
B-1	H.E.C.P.C.	2	54
B-2	Underwater Detection (Augmented)	1	102
B-4(F)	Port Director	1	114
B-4(C)	Harbor Patrol	2	58
B-5(A)	Boat Pools	2	56
B-6	Surface Radar	2	90
B-8	Minesweeping	2	4
B-9	Fleet Moorings	1	-
B-10	Navigational Aids	1	-
C-10	F.P.O. (Augmented)	1	25
D-1	Storage Facilities (Augmented 50%)	1	975
D-3	Tank Farm	1	16
D-11	Drum Filling Plant	1	101
D-13	Cobbler & Tailor Shop	1	11
D-19	Material Recovery Unit	1	33
E-1	Combined AR, AS, AD	2	1528
E-5	Ship Servicing	1	89
E-6	Mobile Amphibious Repair	1	520
E-8	Small Boat Repair	1	68
E-13	Minesweeping Equipment Repair	1	10
E-16	Oxygen Plant	2	24
E-17	Acetylene Plant	1	6
E-18	CO_2 Transfer	1	4
E-19	Typewriter Repair	2	2

ANN I

LION (Cont'd)

	Unit	No. of Units	Personnel
G-2	Hospital (600 bed)	1	193
G-8	Dispensary (25 bed)	3	42
H-14(A)	Tank Farm, MoGas	1	-
J-1	Base Ordnance	1	16
J-2	Machine Gun Component	1	6
J-3	Ammunition Component	20	360
J-5(A)	Torpedo Depot	1	57
J-10	Optical Shop	1	5
J-11(A)	Mine Assembly Depot	1	69
J-11(E)	Depth Charge Testing Component	1	4
J-12(A)	Net Component	1	70
J-13(B)	Degaussing Component	1	21
N-7(A)	Camps (1,000 men)	7	567
N-8(C)	Camp Buildings (Northern)	7	-
N-9	Base Recreation	1	-
N-10	Base Education	1	2
N-12	Laundry	6	30
N-6(A)	Bakery	3	54
P-2	Construction Equipment	1	-
P-8	Port Development	1	-
P-9	Wooden Pier	4	-
P-10	Pontoon Assembly Plant	1	557
P-11	Truck & Equipment Overhaul Plant (Augmented 50%)	1	835
P-12	Fire Fighting Component	1	-
	TOTAL		7,031

P.T. Operating Base

	Unit	No. of Units	Personnel
A-4	Administration	1	10
C-3	Radio	1	10
C-8	Visual	1	-

TOP SECRET

P.T. Operating Base (Cont'd)

	Unit	No. of Units	Personnel
E-11	P.T. Operating Base Repair	1	134
G-10	Dispensary (10 bed)	1	4
J-2	Machine Gun	1	4
J-4(C)	Base Demolition	1	-
J-6(A)	Field Torpedo Circus	1	11
N-1(A)	Camps (250 man)	2	44
N-5(C)	Camp Bldgs. (North)	2	-
N-9	Base Recreation	1	-
P-6(D)	Fire Protection, etc.	1	-
	TOTAL		217

Standard Landing Craft Units (2)

A-3	Administration	2	96
E-10	SLCU Maintenance	2	122
G-8	Dispensary	2	28
N-1(A)	Camps (250 man)	6	132
N-5(C)	Camp Bldgs. (Northern)	6	-
	Boat Personnel		582
	Estimated Additional Boat Crews		2,000
	TOTAL		2,960

Receiving Station (2,000 man)

A-3	Administration	1	48
N-7(A)	Camps (1,000 man)	2	81
N-7(C)	Camp Bldgs. (Northern)	2	-
G-7	Dispensary (50 bed)		70
	TOTAL		199

Navy Communication Units

	Mobile Units	-	375
	Administrative Dets.	-	92
	Garrison Units	-	390
	Camp - Administration	-	130
	FruPac	-	174
	TOTAL		1,161

A16/Ice UNITED STATES PACIFIC FLEET
AND PACIFIC OCEAN AREAS
Headquarters of the Commander in Chief

Serial 000170

21 December 1944

From: Commander in Chief, U.S. Pacific Fleet and
Pacific Ocean Areas.

To : Distribution List.

Subject: Changes to Joint Staff Study, ICEBERG.

Reference: (a) CinCPOA serial 000131 of 25 October 1944.

Enclosures: (A) Appendix G to Joint Staff Study ICEBERG,
with Annex 1, Logistics Measures and
Annex 2, Troop List.
(B) Appendix H to Joint Staff Study ICEBERG,
with Annex 1, Major Forces Required.

1. Enclosures (A) and (B) are forwarded herewith
for insertion in reference (a). Additional annexes to Enclosure (B) will follow. Change Table of Contents to reflect
addition of these appendices.

2. These enclosures will constitute the bases for
logistic preparation and procurement of forces.

FORREST SHERMAN
Deputy Chief of Staff

DISTRIBUTION LIST COPY NO.

CominCh (12)................ 1-12 incl
CNO (2)....................13-14
Com5thFleet (12).......... 15-26 incl
ComGen Tenth Army (35)... 27-51, 159-168 incl
ComPhibsPac (8)........... 52-59 incl
Com5thPhibFor (20)........ 60-79 incl
ComGenPOA (15)............ 80-94 incl
Com3rdFleet (2).......... 95-96
ComGenFMFPac (10)........ 97-106 incl
ComAirPac (4)............ 107-110 incl
ComGenAirFMFPac (2)..... 111-112
ComFwdAreaCentPac (4)... 113-116 incl
ComGenAAFPOA (5)........ 117-121 incl
ComServPac (2).......... 122-123
ComSoPac (2)............ 124-125
CinCSWPA (2)............ 126-127
Com7thFleet (1)......... 128
ComMarGilsArea (1)...... 170
CominPac (1)............ 172

R. E. KEETON,
Assistant
Flag Secretary.

ICEBERG

APPENDIX G

PHASE II

SEIZURE OF IE SHIMA AND OPERATIONS ON OKINAWA SUBSEQUENT TO PHASE I

1. GENERAL

Phase II will be initiated as soon as it is apparent that the necessary combat troops and fire support ships may be diverted from Phase I Operations. This date, W-Day, will be selected by the Commanding General Expeditionary Troops. For planning purposes W-Day is assumed to be D plus 30.

The scheme of maneuver will be designed to provide early seizure of IE SHIMA and initiation of a major airfield development, and occupation of OKINAWA to the extent required for security of our installations on IE SHIMA and establishment of control over the entire island of OKINAWA.

There is insufficient information available at present to warrant the assumption that favorable sites for air or naval development will be secured in the northern portion of OKINAWA.

2. GROUND FORCES

It is estimated that in this phase the seizure of IE SHIMA and OKINAWA southwest of a line joining KAWATA WAN (26° 38' N 128° 9' E) and SHANA WAN (26° 40' N 128° 7' E) will require two corps of two divisions each. One corps will probably be employed in a land advance to the northeast from positions held at the conclusion of Phase I. The other corps will be available for amphibious operations to seize IE SHIMA and MOTOBU PENINSULA and to envelop Japanese forces opposing our land advance.

After the line KAWATA WAN - SHANA WAN has been established, the Commanding General Expeditionary Troops will

proceed to gain control of the remainder of the island to such
a degree as to assure the security of our position. A corps of
three divisions should be sufficient to establish and maintain
this control throughout OKINAWA JIMA and IE SHIMA, thus making
it possible to release the remaining divisions for third phase
operations.

As soon as it becomes evident that Japanese forces
have been disorganized and enemy capabilities reduced to
passive resistance the number of divisions in the OKINAWA -
IE SHIMA Area may be reduced to two.

3. AIR FORCES

IE SHIMA will be developed as an air base for the
operation of two heavy bomb groups and two long range fighter
groups. It is estimated that these fields will be operational
for fighters by W $\neq$ 10 and for bombers by W $\neq$ 50.

Alternate

The tactical situation in Phase I may require early
capture and initial development of IE SHIMA, with forces provided
for Phase I, in order to provide additional shore based air
support. In this case the two fighter groups, one Army and one
Marine, with supporting and service troops, scheduled for
installation on OKINAWA will be utilized for this contingency.
If so used, the facilities acquired at IE SHIMA will make
acceptable a delay in activation of two airfields on OKINAWA.
If such a diversion of forces is made those listed herein will
be available for activation of airfields on OKINAWA.

4. NAVAL FORCES

Upon completion of Phase I, it will be desirable for
reasons of security to retain in the immediate area only those
units of the fire support force as will be required for the

prosecution of Phase II. It is estimated that this will comprise about one half of the fire support force initially committed. This reduced force will be available to support the shore-to-shore operation against IE SHIMA, and the advance northward on OKINAWA as required.

It is expected that a covering force of reduced strength, carriers and battleships, will be required to remain within striking distance of OKINAWA throughout Phase II and for an indefinite period thereafter in order to prevent enemy surface ship raids, to augment the shore based air defenses, and to strike adjacent enemy positions.

Landing craft will be retained in sufficient numbers to implement the shore-to-shore assault on IE SHIMA, to provide means for shore-to-shore amphibious assaults in the northern part of OKINAWA and for use in unloading cargo ships supporting the operation.

No naval facilities other than small craft repair and minor harbor services are planned for IE SHIMA. It is expected that various bays and inlets will be discovered in the northern portion of OKINAWA which will be suitable for PT bases and for other small craft anchorages. It is not intended that any provision be made at the present time for naval shore establishment or nets except in NAKAGUSUKU WAN, KERAMA RETTO and NAHA; destroyer mooring buoys and secondary navigation buoys however should be available for several small craft anchorages which are expected to become available.

5. FORCES REQUIRED

a. Ground Force   From

IE SHIMA

Assault

1 Division   Phase I

	Garrison	From
	1 RCT	Assault force
	1 Bn AAA Gun (reinf) (Army)	

OKINAWA

As directed by ComGen
10th Army   Phase I

b. Air Forces

IE SHIMA

Garrison

2 Gps VBH (Army)	1 PALAU - 1 U.S.
2 Gps VF (Army)	U.S.
4 Air service groups (Sp)(Army)	1 PALAU - 3 U.S.
2 Avn Engr Bns	MARIANAS if available, or U.S.
1 A.W. Squadron	

c. Naval Forces

Covering Force	3 CV 3 CL
	1 CVL 18 DD
	2-3 BB
	2 CB or 3 CA
Fire Support Force	4 OBB 18 DD
	2 CA 9 LCI(G)
	2 CL
Air Support Force	None
Assault Shipping	30 LST 50 LCM
	36 LCI(L) 150 LCVP
	20 LSM
Base Defense & Support Force	None

d. Service Units - See Annex 2.

ICEBERG

ANNEX 1 TO APPENDIX G

LOGISTIC MEASURES - PHASE II

1.   GENERAL

In addition to the logistic measures discussed in Appendix E to Phase I the following factors applicable to Phase II are significant.

2.   FACTS AFFECTING LOGISTICS

  a. Terrain

IE SHIMA lies on the northwest side of OKINAWA at a distance of three miles from the tip of MOTOBU PENINSULA. It is a limestone island, roughly oval in form, five miles long and two miles wide. This island contains approximately 5500 acres, nearly all of which area is sufficiently level for development purposes. The island is topped by a nearly level plateau which averages about 150 feet above sea level. This area appears to have been intensively cultivated. Near the eastern end is a volcanic plug about 555 feet high called IKOSUKU YAMA or "Sugar Loaf" at the south base of which lies a large village. A major air base development has been undertaken by the enemy.

  b. Water Supply

It is believed that an ample supply of water can be developed by drilling wells in the center of the island down to approximately sea level. In the case of this island a depth of 150 - 200 feet is indicated. The enemy has probably developed a water supply system which might be salvaged.

  c. Harbors

There is no sheltered anchorage area adjoining the island. Berthing facilities are few and concentrated near the village on the southeast shore. This is the leeward side of the islands for the prevailing winds of northerly directions. These facilities are located on embayments in the coral reef on the Southeast shore. They appear to be of solid construction. The wharf on the west side is not yet completed.

It does not appear that the water alongside these structures is deep enough to accommodate anything but small boats or barges at high tide. There is no protection for small craft against southerly blows and it seems not unlikely that the samll developed harbor at TOGUIGHI Harbor (dredged to $6\frac{1}{2}$ ft. in 1939) may serve for the transshipment of supplies for the support of the IE SHIMA Air Base, particularly during a period of winds from the south.

In view of the difficulty or impossibility of providing protected berthing for large ships here lightering must be considered as the only practicable means of supply. Tanker moorings could be installed on the south side of the island for delivery of fuel by submarine hose.

d. Beach Capacities

The southern and eastern shores have four firm, coral and sand beaches from 9 to 35 yards wide and 125 to 900 yards long. The remainder of the island is bounded by rocky sea-cliffs.

A fringing reef 360 to 720 yards wide with scattered coral heads, and without channels, borders the island.

Moderate slopes lead inland from all beaches, rising about 20 feet to a border of casuarina trees. Scattered clumps of trees form two rather distant lines between the casuarinas and the airfield.

Interruption of the tree fringe behind the beaches, and breaks in the slope offer good exits in addition to the roads and trails leading inland from all beaches. These roads join with the predominantly east-west road net which links all portions of the island. Several of the roads appear to be about six to eight feet wide and unsurfaced, although several such as the southern coast road, 135 yards inland, are about 12 feet wide and coral surfaced.

It is estimated that the above beaches will afford unloading capacities totaling 75,000 MT/Mo.

3.   CONTEMPLATED DEVELOPMENT

    a. Airfield Development

    IE SHIMA is well adapted to the construction of flying fields because of its relatively level terrain. Approach conditions are over water and are ideal. Much enemy construction here can conveniently be used again.

    Photographic coverage shows four parallel runways which can be made ready in a comparatively short time.

    Field No. 1. Photographic coverage of 10 October 1944 showed that this runway was cleared by the enemy without any grading.

    Field No. 2. The runway was graded and surfaced to a length of approximately 5000 feet on 10 October 1944. A cross runway 4300 feet long, together with taxiways and hardstands, had also been completed at that date, and can probably be used again. It is planned to increase the main runway to 7000 feet for use by VBH.

    Field No. 3. As of 10 October 1944 one runway at this field was operational for a length of approximately 5100 feet. A taxiway system with hardstands was partly completed, and a second runway at an angle seems to have been under construction. It is proposed to recondition the present runway for fighter planes without adding to its length.

    Field No. 4. This field will be of entirely new construction at the east end of the island. It is to have a runway of 5500 feet in length.

    Ready Dates. Estimated ready dates for airfields on IE SHIMA are tabulated below. These dates are predicated on:

    (1) Employment of three (3) Aviation Engineer Battalions.
    (2) Availability of the sites for commencing work by W ∤ 5.

	Field No.			
	1	2	3	4
Operational for VF (4500' runway)	W∤10	W∤10	W∤50	
Operational for VBH (6000' runway)	W∤90	W∤50		

- 79 -

Final completion of the entire development is estimated at W ≠ 230, and will provide for 5500' runways for VF and 7000' runways for VBH Fields.

b. Naval Facilities

No facilities for support of Naval Units other than small craft is contemplated.

c. Harbor Development and Waterfront Facilities

Installation of tanker and AvGas and MoGas barge moorings off southern shore for delivery of AvGas and MoGas by submarine line.

Transshipment from OKINAWA utilizing small craft will not be practicable during the early stages of development. Personnel and equipment for unloading AKs and APs from moorings at IE SHIMA must be provided during this period. Subsequent to the establishment of adequate port facilities on OKINAWA and when the inbound traffic on that island has passed its peak, transshipment from OKINAWA to IE SHIMA in small craft may be resorted to and some labor on IE SHIMA may be relieved. At this time the amount of labor required on OKINAWA will be increased accordingly.

Installation of AK moorings off southern shore with utilization of individual ship protective nets.

Installation of aids to navigation.

4. MEDICAL FACILITIES AND EVACUATION POLICY

a. Estimate of Casualties:

Dead and missing	800
Local hospitalization	800
Requiring evacuation	2,400
Total Casualties	4,000

b. Evacuation

Casualties will be evacuated by available AHs, APHs and APA to the MARIANAS. If LSTs or smaller vessels are utilized, casualties will be evacuated to OKINAWA for further evacuation by surface or air.

<u>c</u>. <u>Hospitalization</u>

Initially, hospitalization will be provided by mobile hospital units. Subsequent to the assault phase, hospitalization will be provided as directed in the base development plan, and as indicated in the garrison troop list.

<u>d</u>. <u>Medical Care for Civilians</u>

Assault: Estimated casualties, 700. Requiring hospitalization, 350. During the assault phase, civilian casualties will be handled by medical units designated for Military Government, assigned to the assault division. After the assault phase, civilians will be cared for by medical units designated for Military Government. Civilian casualties will not be evacuated from the island.

Garrison: Medical care of civilians by units assigned to garrison forces.

5.   <u>SUPPORT OF LAND BASED FORCES</u>

<u>a</u>. <u>Method of Supply</u>

The primary method of supply will be by direct maintenance shipments from the West Coast.

When practicable the supply of Assault and Garrison Forces will be by utilization of LCTs, LSTs and other small craft from the port of NAHA or other accessible loading points on OKINAWA. Due to lack of facilities and heavy requirements for OKINAWA, transshipment may not be practicable in the early stages.

Provision should be made for AK moorings to unload at IE SHIMA any ships of regularly scheduled maintenance shipments, or any other cargo ship, assigned to the support of this operation.

<u>b</u>. <u>Responsibilities for Supply, Levels of Supply and Supplies to Accompany Troops</u>

The same general provisions as obtained in Phase I will apply in Phase II.

<u>c</u>. <u>Shipping Instructions</u>

A separate shipping designation for IE SHIMA will be assigned to

facilitate direct maintenance shipments to this port.

6.   MILITARY GOVERNMENT

    a. Assault Phase

During the assault phase Military Government functions in IE SHIMA will be performed by the Military Government detachments, including medical, which are regularly assigned to the assault division.

    b. Garrison Phase

Upon completion of the assault phase, the Military Government detachments assigned to the assault division will revert to the control of the garrison commander. These detachments will be augmented when practicable by one Military Government Camp Unit to be carried in garrison shipping. This unit is in addition to those previously provided for Phase I.

7.   SERVICE TROOPS

Unless otherwise indicated in Annex 2 to Appendix G - Phase II, all service units will be in addition to those listed for Phase I.

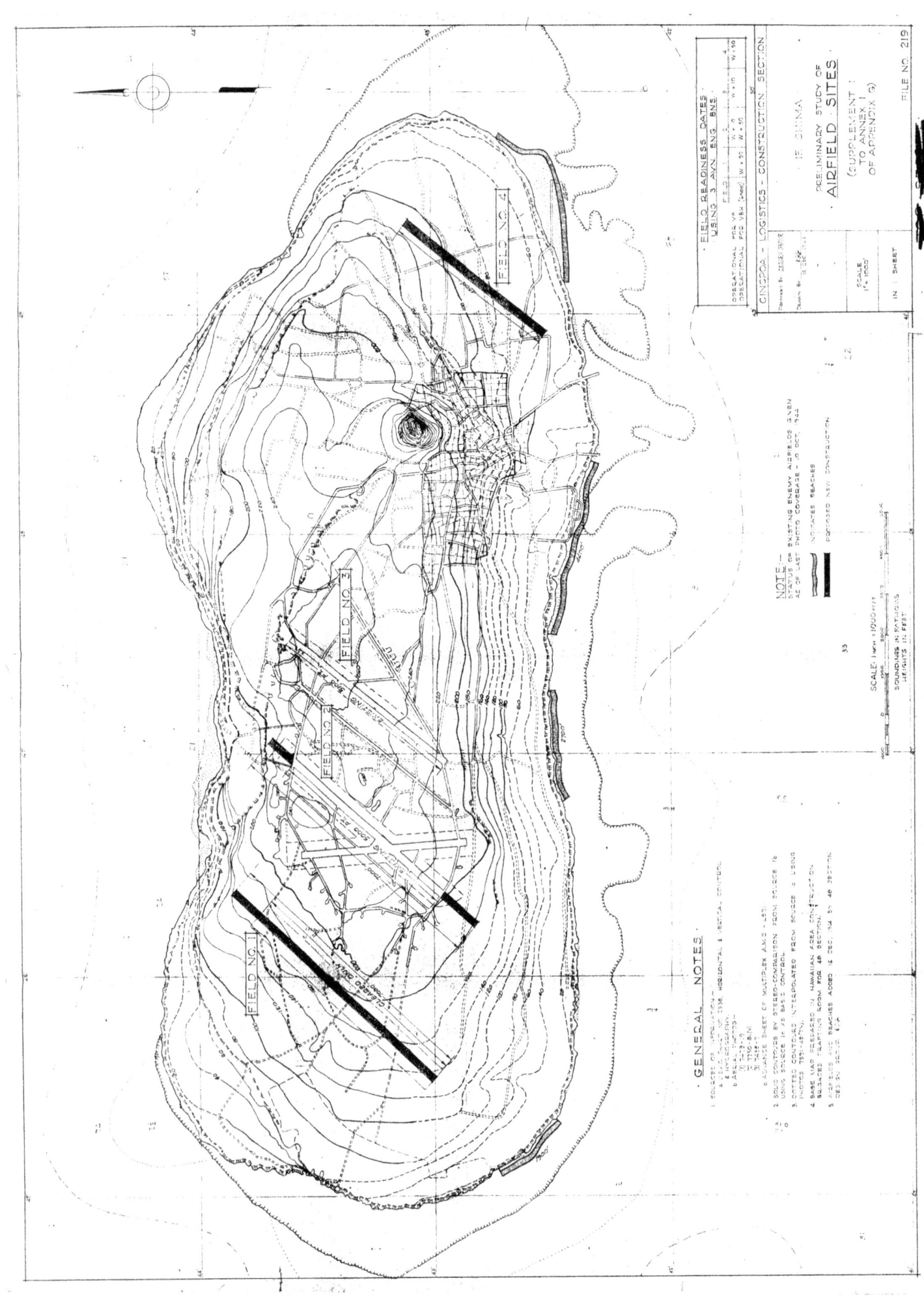

ICEBERG
ANNEX 2 TO APPENDIX G
TROOP LIST - PHASE II

UNIT	T/O	ASSAULT Army	Navy	Marine	GARRISON Army	Navy	Marine	Mounting From	REMARKS
Division (Reinforced) Amphibious trained and equipped for independent operation including Garrison Beach Party.	-	1 - 24,500			1 - 5000			Phase I	One (1) RCT with appropriate medical units in Civil Affairs Team will remain in garrison phase. Additional Civil Affairs Team will arrive later.
JASCO		24,500	500		5000	200			
Civil Affairs Team			500			200			
Note: Unless otherwise indicated all units will mount from U.S.									
AVIATION									
VBH Groups	1-117 1-37 1-12			2 - 3564 2 - 2274				PALAU (1)	
VF Groups									
Serv.Group Spec	1-452 1-457 1-458			4 - 2632				PALAU (1) U.S. (3)	
Aviation Sqdn	1-999			1 - 252			1-230	230	
Weather Detachment	-			1 - 15					
Base Hq & A.B. Sqdn	1-422			2 - 202					
Air Warning Sqdn	B-691								
ANTI-AIRCRAFT									
Hq & Hq Btry, Gp	44-12			1 - 73					
Gun Bn Sem (A), plus 2 -	44-115			1 - 631					
Gun Btries Sem (A)	44-117			2 - 248					
AW Bn Sem, plus	44-125			1 - 787					
2 - AW Btries	44-127			2 - 328					
								8939	

-83-

UNIT	T/O	ASSAULT Army	ASSAULT Navy	ASSAULT Marine	GARRISON Army	GARRISON Navy	GARRISON Marine	Mounting From	REMARKS
ANTI-AIRCRAFT (Cont'd)									
S/L Btry (B)(less radar), plus	44-138	1- 147							
1 - Plat (less radar)	44-138	1- 52							
FINANCE									
Disb Sec (AB-BG-CA-DC types)	14-500	1- 22	2,265		22				
MEDICAL									
Evacuation Hospital (SM) 400-bed	8-581	1-246			1- 246				Departs with Assault Div. less nurses. /Nurses
Station Hospital 500-bed	8-560				1- 337				
Malaria Survey Unit (FB)	8-500				1- 13				
Malaria Control Unit (FA)	8-500	246			1- 12				
					362				
ORDNANCE									
Medium Maint Co	9-9				1- 169				Only 3rd Ech. Maint.
Ord Dep Co	9-57				1- 186				
Ord Med Auto Maint Co	9-127				1- 120				Only 3rd Ech. Maint.
Bomb Disposal Sqd	9-179				1- 7				
Ord Ammo Co Avn	9-17				1- 179				
Ord Supply and Maint Co Avn	9-417				1- 78				Only 3rd Ech. Maint.
					739				
SIGNAL									
Communication Unit						1-100			
AACS Det	11-217				1- 30				
Sig Det Avn	11-500				1- 100				
Gp Hq (Augmented)	11-500				1- 48				
Sig Serv Co	11-500				1- 250				
Sig Cons Co Hv	11-67				1- 204				
					632				

UNIT	T/O	ASSAULT			GARRISON			Mounting From	REMARKS
		Army	Navy	Marine	Army	Navy	Marine		
QUARTERMASTER									
Hq & Hq Det QM Bn	10-536				2- 54				2 - Med Dets of 2 Off & 8 EM each (Attchd).
QM Service Co	10-67				2- 426				Based on moving 20,000 MT per month.
QM Laundry Co SM (less 2 Plats)	10-167				1- 144				
QM Bakery Plat	10-147				2- 68				
QM Graves Reg Plat	10-297				1- 23				
QM Depot Co, Supply (less 1 Plat)	10-227				2- 134				
QM Salvage Coll Plat	10-187				1- 62				
QM Salvage Rep Plat	10-237				1- 88				
QM Truck Co	10-57				1- 134				
					1,133				
ENGINEERS									
Engr Avn Bn	5-415				3- 2295				
Water Supply Plat	5-67				1- 38				
Engr Const Bn	5-75				1- 901				
Engr Dump Truck Co	5-88				3- 342				
Const Bn (Navy)	F-1					3576			
ADJUTANT GENERAL									
Base Post Office	12-605				1- 20	1- 558			
Base Censorship Det	-				1- 20	558			
					40				
MILITARY POLICE									
Military Police Co, Avn	19-217				1- 104				
					104				
TRANSPORTATION CORPS									
Port Cos	55-117				2- 460				
Hq & Hq Det Port Bn	55-116				1- 34				
					494				

This is considered adequate if the supplies to be handled do not exceed 40,000 M.T. per month above normal maintenance for garrison.

UNIT	T/O	ASSAULT			GARRISON			Mounting From	REMARKS
		Army	Navy	Marine	Army	Navy	Marine		
NAVAL UNITS									
GROPAC Boat Pool	—		500			717			1 - 367 1 - 350
TOTALS	—	24746			23307	1575	230		
GRAND TOTAL ALL SERVICES		ASSAULT 25246			GARRISON 25112				

-86-

A16/ICE

UNITED STATES PACIFIC FLEET
AND PACIFIC OCEAN AREAS
Headquarters of the Commander in Chief

Serial 0005024 *Superceded by Annex H, dated 14 April 1945*   28 February 1945

~~TOP SECRET~~

From: Commander in Chief, U. S. Pacific Fleet and Pacific Ocean
            Areas.
To :   DISTRIBUTION LIST.

Subject: Change to Joint Staff Study, ICEBERG.

Reference: (a) Cincpoa Top Secret serial 000131 of 25 October 1944.

Enclosure: (A) Appendix H to Joint Staff Study, ICEBERG with Annex
                1, Major Forces Required.

    1.   The following changes should be made to reference (a):

        (a) Remove and destroy by burning pages 87-105 inclusive.

        (b) Insert new pages 87-98 inclusive (Enclosure (A)).

    2.   Corrected Annexes 2 and 3 to Appendix H will be issued at
an early date.

                                        C. H. McMORRIS,
                                        Chief of Staff.

DISTRIBUTION

                                        Copy No.

CominCh (12)* ....   1-12 incl.
CNO (2)   13-14
Com5thFleet (12) ....   15-26 incl.
ComGen10thArmy (36) ....   27-51 incl., 129, 159-168 incl.
ComPhibsPac (8) ....   52-59 incl.
Com5thPhibFor (20) ....   60-79 incl.
ComGenPOA (15) ....   80-94 incl.
Com3rdFleet (2)   95-96
ComGenFMFPac (10) ....   97-106 incl.
ComAirPac (4) ....   107-110 incl.
ComGenAirFMFPac (2)   111-112
ComFwdAreaCentPac (4) ....   113-116 incl.
ComGenAAFPOA (5) ....   117-121 incl.
ComServPac (2)   122-123
ComSoPac (2)   124-125
CinCSWPA (2)   126-127
Com7thFleet (1)   128
ComMarGilsArea (1)   170
ComNABs, Navy No. 3256 (1)   171
CominPac (1)   172
    * Includes copies for War Department

O. L. THORNE,
Flag Secretary.

APP H
Phase III

ICEBERG

APPENDIX H

PHASE III

SEIZURE AND DEVELOPMENT OF ADDITIONAL POSITIONS

1. GENERAL

  a. Objectives

       Phase III will comprise the capture of additional islands
in order to extend our air bombardment and blockade of JAPAN. Although
reconnaissance is incomplete it appears that the only islands in the
RYUKYUS susceptible of extensive development are MIYAKO and KIKAI. MIYAKO
will be captured and developed primarily as a base for VLR aircraft. KIKAI,
after capture, will be developed as an advanced base for fighters. It is
expected that lack of forces, particularly Army service troops, will preclude the seizure of either of these objectives until such time as additional service units become available in the Pacific Ocean Areas.

       Assuming that the necessary service troops are available,
the operations comprising Phase III may conform to the following approximate
time schedule, L Day being the day of initial landing on OKINAWA:

MIYAKO	A Day	L plus 90
KIKAI	F Day	L plus 120

       MIYAKO is to be captured first because of the greater
length of time required to develop VLR bases and in order to conform as
nearly as possible to the anticipated availability dates of VLR wings.

       KIKAI, being close to other enemy air bases in the AMAMI
Group and a relatively short distance from JAPAN, should be captured after
MIYAKO in order to allow a longer period for attrition of Japanese air forces.

       Delays in the availability of service troops beyond the
dates indicated above will impose corresponding delays in the seizure of the
objectives.

b. Ground Forces

The V Amphibious Corps (3rd, 4th, and 5th Marine Divisions) is designated as the assault force for the capture of MIYAKO. The 3rd Marine Division and the Corps troops will be mounted in the MARIANAS area, and the 4th and 5th Marine Divisions in the HAWAIIAN area. Rehearsals will take place in the mounting areas.

One infantry division (reinforced) will be designated for the capture of KIKAI from the combat troops allocated to ICEBERG. Mounting and rehearsals will take place in the OKINAWA GUNTO.

c. Air Forces

Preliminary bombing of MIYAKO will be accomplished by the coordinated efforts of fast carriers, the Tactical Air Force at OKINAWA, and heavy bombers from LUZON. Direct air support of the assault will be provided by escort carriers.

Preliminary bombardment and direct air support of the assault on KIKAI will be provided by the Tactical Air Force, assisted as required by elements of the Fast Carrier Task Forces.

The primary function of the Fast Carrier Task Forces will be to cover the operations of Phase III by conducting continuing attacks on strategic and tactical targets on the Japanese mainland. These attacks will be coordinated with operations of the 20th Air Force and will be intensified against KYUSHU and western HONSHU during the movements of assault shipping in order to provide strategic support.

Transport carriers will transport aircraft spares, pilots, and air crews to the combat areas for replenishment of CV's, CVL's, and CVE's. In addition, they will be required to transport certain garrison aircraft units to be designated.

<u>d</u>.   Naval Forces

Phase III will require assault shipping sufficient to mount three divisions, construction forces for early activation of airfields, and ground echelon and service units of initial air garrison. Three transport squadrons will be necessary to mount the V Amphibious Corps for the seizure of MIYAKO. The capture of KIKAI will be conducted as a shore-to-shore movement, using landing ships and landing craft exclusively.

In view of the reduced strength of the Japanese fleet and our strategic position in LUZON and OKINAWA, it is believed that three fast carrier task groups will be sufficient covering force for these operations.

Escort carriers will provide air cover for assault shipping during the movement to MIYAKO and close air support during the landing operations. Three close air support units or a total of twelve CVE's will be required. Shore based aviation should be capable of providing adequate close air support for the capture of KIKAI and the employment of escort carriers is not considered necessary for this purpose.

The total fire support force will be utilized in the MIYAKO operation. This force may be reduced for the assault on KIKAI.

2.   <u>MIYAKO - Phase III c.</u> (There is no Phase III a. or III b.)

<u>a</u>.   General Discussion

MIYAKO has been selected as an objective in order to acquire additional airfield sites for the following purposes:

(1) To provide a base relatively close to JAPAN for VLR aircraft.

(2) To provide an offensive air base to complete the neutralization of enemy positions in FORMOSA.

(3) As a defensive southern outpost to provide greater security for our position in OKINAWA.

The capture, occupation, defense, and development of MIYAKO will be initiated as soon as the necessary service troops become available and the necessary assault shipping and combat units can be released from other operations.

Maximum naval covering and fire support forces available will be employed

During the assault phase the Commander Expeditionary Force will be responsible for initiating the development of MIYAKO. Upon completion of the assault phase the Commanding General, Tenth Army, will be responsible for the shore defenses, administration, and logistic support of the island.

b. Ground Forces

The estimated strength of the Japanese forces on MIYAKO is one infantry division (less one RCT) and two independent mixed brigades with supporting and service troops, totalling 20,000 - 22,000. The 1940 civil population was 60,786. A corps of three reinforced divisions is considered a suitable assault force. One division, to be provided from the assault force until a relief division is available, will be required for the defense of the island. Assault and garrison forces are listed in Annex 1 to this Appendix.

The coast of MIYAKO is nearly everywhere precipitous. The most extensive beaches border the peninsulas forming JUNK BAY. Though these beaches are backed by relatively low, rough, wooded escarpments, access inland is probably less obstructed than from any other beaches. The small islands of YERABU, SHIMOJI, and KURUMA which lie from 1-1/2 to 4-1/2 miles off JUNK BAY afford possible positions for emplacement of artillery to support the landing forces. The three existing enemy airfields are grouped on an arc about JUNK BAY, at a distance of from 1 to 2 miles therefrom. The scheme of maneuver will provide for the seizure of the three small off-lying islands en A-1 day, and the emplacement of artillery to support the main landings on A Day. Two divisions in the assault will land in JUNK BAY area in order to seize the three existing airfields. The attack will then be continued to capture the remainder of the island. A third division will be held initially in floating reserve.

c.   Air Forces

Prior to our attack MIYAKO will have been subjected to
repeated air attacks by both shore-based and carrier aviation in order to
neutralize its air bases as a safeguard for our position in OKINAWA. About
A-15 an intensive air attack will be initiated to destroy defensive installations. The Fast Carrier Task Groups may assist in the preliminary bombardment of the target but will cover the operation by conducting strikes against
strategic and tactical targets in KYUSHU and HONSHU. The Southwest Pacific
Area air forces will be requested to assist in this operation by the neutralization of airfields in FORMOSA and by extensive heavy bomber attacks on
MIYAKO. Direct air support of the assault and neutralization of adjacent
supporting bases will be provided by escort carriers.

Four airfields will be constructed to accommodate two wings
(8 groups) of very long range bombers, two fighter groups, one night fighter
squadron, one Marine torpedo bomber squadron for anti-submarine patrol.

Air forces are listed in Annex 1 to this appendix.

d.   Naval Forces

Three transport squadrons will be provided from new construction
to mount the V Amphibious Corps for this operation. Two transport squadrons
will assemble in HAWAII on A-46 to mount the 4th and 5th MarDivs; and one
transport squadron in the MARIANAS on A-36 to mount the 3rd Mar Div.

All available fire support units will be required in order
to effect maximum destruction of enemy defenses prior to the assault. The
fire support units will be assembled in OKINAWA and will precede the assault
force to the objective by at least five days. The minesweeping group should
depart OKINAWA with the fire support group.

Naval forces are listed in Annex 1 to this appendix.

PART II

3. KIKAI - Phase III d.

    a. General Discussion

        The second objective for Phase III is KIKAI. This objective
is selected in order to acquire additional airfield sites for the following
purposes:

        To operate fighters for escort, and for air defense to the
north of OKINAWA.

        To neutralize other bases in the AMAMI Group.

        The seizure of this objective will be conducted as a shore-
to-shore movement using amphibious craft and employing assault forces released from active operations in the OKINAWA area. Naval covering and fire
support forces will be retained as required from the MIYAKO operation to
support the assault on KIKAI.

    b. Ground Forces.

        The estimated strength of the Japanese forces in the AMAMI
Group is one division, one independent mixed brigade, and one independent
mixed regiment with supporting and service troops, totaling 21,700 - 23,700.
Of this total it is estimated that 3,500 are on KIKAI. The 1940 civil population was 18, 184. In view of the enemy combat strength in the AMAMI Group,
and his capability of quickly reinforcing KIKAI, it is estimated that one
reinforced infantry division should constitute the assault force. One
infantry division will be required for the defense of the island. Assault
and garrison forces are listed in Annex 1 to this appendix.

        The only potential landing beaches are at SOMACHI HAKUCHI
and at SHITOOKE on the northeast coast, and at WAN and AGARE on the southwest coast. Weather permitting, the northeast coast is considered the better
landing area. The scheme of maneuver will provide for landings on the northeast coast, or alternately, at WAN and AGARE in the event of unfavorable
weather conditions on the northeast coast.

c.   Air Forces

Air operations against KIKAI will be continuous after our establishment in OKINAWA, in order to maintain its neutralization. When the neutralization of MIYAKO and the SAKASHIMA Group is taken over by the escort carrier force, the entire offensive effort of the Tactical Air Force will be available for employment against KIKAI. KIKAI will be kept under continuous attack to destroy its defensive installations as well as to neutralize its airfields.

The proximity of KIKAI to KYUSHU makes it inadvisable to expose CVE's to attack from that major air center unless previous operations of the Fast Carrier Task Forces and the shore based aviation has resulted in an appreciable decline of Japanese offensive air capabilities. The short distance of 155 miles from OKINAWA to KIKAI will enable shore based air forces to provide convoy cover, direct air support, and combat air patrol over our forces at the objective. To augment the available shore based air strength during this period, units of the Strategic Air Force will be attached to the Tactical Air Force as required.

Subsequent to our landing and until local air defenses are established, air defense will have to be provided by combat air patrols from OKINAWA and continuous attacks on enemy air bases in KYUSHU by both shore and carrier based aviation.

KIKAI will be developed to provide a base for four fighter groups, two night fighter squadrons, and one Marine torpedo bomber squadron. Air forces are listed in Annex 1 to this appendix.

d.   Naval Forces

The assault shipping for Phase III-d will consist exclusively of landing ships and landing craft which have been retained from the MIYAKO assault. It is expected that these will be assembled in OKINAWA where the assault force will be mounted.

The fire support force will consist of 6 OBB, 3 CA, 3 CL, 18 DD, 9 LCI(G), and 9 LCI(M) from the force used in the MIYAKO assault.

The same covering force employed in Phase III-c will be used to support the operations against KIKAI.

Close air support will be provided by shore based aircraft from OKINAWA; therefore, no close naval air support units will be necessary.

Naval forces are listed in Annex 1 to this appendix.

ICEBERG

Annex 1 to Appendix H

MAJOR FORCES REQUIRED — PHASE III

1. GROUND FORCES

Assault Forces	MIYAKO	KIKAI
Marine Amphibious Corps of 3 MarDivs (V Amphibious Corps)	1	
Infantry Division, amphibiously trained		1
Tank Battalion (medium)		1
Engineer Combat Bn		3
Hq & Hq Co, Engr Gp		1
Amphibious Tractor Bn		3
Amphibious Tank Bn		1
Amphibious Truck Co		2
JASCO's		1
Chemical Co (motorized)		1

Garrison Forces	MIYAKO	KIKAI
Infantry Division	1	1
Tank Company (medium)	1	1
AAA Gun Bn	3	3
AAA A/W Bn	4	3
AAA S/L Bn (— 1 battery)	1	1
Hq & Hq Btry AAA Gp	2	2
155-mm Gun (CA) Bn	2	2
Hq & Hq Btry CA Gp	1	1
MP Battalion	1	1
Hq & Hq Btry AAA Brig	1	1

2. **AIR FORCES**

Garrison		From

MIYAKO

Army –	2 Wings VLR (includes 2 Wg Hq and 8 groups, with supporting troops)	U. S.
	1 Sq Photo Recon, VLR	GUAM
	1 Hq & Hq – Sv Co, Engr Avn Regt	CentPac
	2 Groups Fighters	U. S.
	1 Sq Night Fighters	U. S.
Marine –	1 Sq VMTB	CentPac
	1 Sq Air Warning	HAWAII

KIKAI

Army –	1 Hq Fighter Wing	U. S.
	4 Groups VF	1 – HAWAII 3 – U. S.
	2 Sq VF(N)	1 – IWO JIMA 1 – SAIPAN
Marine –	1 Sq VMTB	CentPac
	1 Sq Air Warning	HAWAII

3. **NAVAL FORCES**

Covering Force	MIYAKO	KIKAI
CV	8	8
CVL	4	4
BB	6	6
CA	6	6
CL	4	4
CL(AA)	4	4
DD	62	62

	MIYAKO	KIKAI
Fire Support Force		
OBB	10	6
CB	2	0
CA	10	3
CL	4	3
DD	27	18
LCI(G)	9	9
LCI(M)	9	9
Air Support Force		
CVE	12	0
DD	18	0
Assault Shipping		
AGC	3	1
APA	45	0
AKA	18	0
LSV	3	0
LSD	3	2
LST	100	30
LCT	20	10
LCI(L)	0	36
LSM	30	20
DD	27	9
DE	12	6
DMS	6	4
APD	6	12
AM	6	4
YMS	12	12
PC	12	6

Garrison

Base Supported	MIYAKO	KIKAI
LCT	10	10
LCM	60	20
LCVP	20	10
YMT	4	4
YTB	4	0
YNg	2	2

Fleet Supported		
DD	9	9
DE	0	6
PC	6	6
SC	6	6
LST	10	4
LCI(L)	18	18
YMS	6	6
AGP	0	2
PT	0	24
AD	1	0
ARL	1	1
AN	4	4

Cincpac File
A16/Ice

Serial 000211

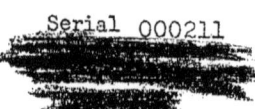

UNITED STATES PACIFIC FLEET
AND PACIFIC OCEAN AREAS
Headquarters of the Commander in Chief

COPY NO. 15

5 February 1945

From: Commander in Chief, U.S. Pacific Fleet and Pacific Ocean
            Areas.
To: Distribution List.

Subject: Changes to Joint Staff Study, ICEBERG.

References: (a) Cincpoa serial 000170 of 21 December 1944, ICEBERG
                Phase II and III.
            (b) Cincpoa serial 000131 of 25 October 1944, ICEBERG
                Phase I.

Enclosures: (A) Annex 2 to Appendix H, Joint Staff Study ICEBERG, Logistic
                Measures Phase III.
            (B) Annex 3 to Appendix H, Joint Staff Study ICEBERG, Troop
                List Phase III.

    1.   Reference (a) stated additional annexes to Appendix H to subject
Study would follow.

    2.   Enclosures (A) and (B) are forwarded herewith for insertion in
reference (b). Change Table of Contents to reflect addition of these annexes.

                                           J. H. TOWERS
                                      Deputy Cincpac & Cincpoa

DISTRIBUTION LIST

CominCh   (12)   ComGenAAFPOA   (5)
CNO   (2)   ComServPac   (2)
Com5thFleet   (12)   ComSoPac   (2)
ComGen10thArmy   (35)   CinCSWPA   (2)
ComPhibsPac   (8)   Com7thFleet   (1)
Com5thPhibFor   (20)   ComMarGilsArea   (1)
ComGenPOA   (15)   CominPac   (1)
Com3rdFleet   (2)
ComGenFMFPac   (10)
ComAirPac   (4)
ComGenAirFMFPac   (2)
ComFwdAreaCentPac   (4)

                R. E. KEETON
                Ass't Flag Secretary

1. GENERAL

    In addition to the logistic measures discussed in Appendix E to Phase I
and Annex 1 to Appendix G, Phase II, the following factors applicable to Phase
III are significant.

2. OPERATIONAL REQUIREMENTS

    The concept of operations requires:

    <u>a</u>. on OKINO DAITO JIMA the early availability and installation of equipment
    and personnel for a LORAN station.

    <u>b</u>. On KUME SHIMA, MIYAKO JIMA and KIKAI JIMA rapid construction of additional
    airdrome facilities.

3. FACTS AFFECTING LOGISTICS

    <u>a</u>. Distances of the objectives from points shown are as follows, in nautical
    miles:

	OKINO	KUME	MIYAKO	KIKAI
OKINAWA (NAHA)	207	48	170	248
IWO JIMA	567	835	880	655
GUAM	1015	1277	1287	1215
SAIPAN	996	1265	1300	1190
ULITHI	990	1221	1200	1235
MANUS	1814	2061	1998	2075
LEYTE	900	945	845	1110
FORMOSA	546	296	209	515
KYUSHU	415	375	474	175
SHANGHAI	677	413	439	485

    Supplement 1 to this Annex shows the relative position and size of the
    four objectives.

    <u>b</u>. PHYSICAL SURVEY

        (1) OKINO DAITO SHIMA (see Supplement 2 to Annex 2 of Appendix H) is
        roughly triangular, approximately 5000 feet in its greatest

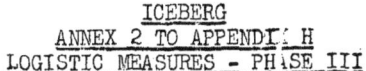

dimension, and contains .45 square miles or 290 acres. It is a flat-topped coral formation bounded by steep rocky cliffs sloping 80 feet to the sea. Phosphate deposits are being exploited at the northwest end of the island and there is evidence of cane cultivation. No high standard roads have been built but a narrow gauge railroad links the northern phosphate diggings with the western coast. The barracks of the phosphate workers are the only settlement; population in 1938 was 2,000.

(2) KUME SHIMA (see Supplement 3 to Annex 2 of Appendix H) is about eight miles long, contains 21 square miles, and is largely undeveloped. Its topography varies from small coastal plains to sand dunes, terraces and hills, some of which rise to 1,000 feet. Agriculture is the only significant industry. A 9-foot road circles the island, generally following the coast, and a number of minor roads cross the interior, but there are no railroads. Of several settlements GIMA, on the southwest coast, is the largest. The Island's population in 1940 was 13,400.

(3) MIYAKO JIMA (see Supplement 4 to Annex 2 of Appendix H) is a triangular island twenty miles on its longest, the northeast, coast and 65 square miles in area. Most of it is low and flat, but there are six roughly parallel ridges, 300 to 400 feet in elevation, with steep eastern and gentle western slopes. No sizeable industry other than agriculture is reported. Roads of 9 feet or greater width follow the western shore and link it with the southern and eastern parts of the island. There is no evidence of a railroad. Of numerous scattered settlements HIRARA on the west coast is the largest, having nearly half of the Island's total 1940 population of 60,000.

(4) KIKAI SHIMA (see Supplement 5 to Annex 2 of Appendix H) is eight miles long, three miles in its greatest width, and has an area of 22 square miles. A number of plateaus slope gently to the north and east to an elevation of nearly 700 feet. Sand dunes occur in the western end. There is no industry of importance. A minor perimeter

road circles the island and a main road connects the two principal towns, SOMACHI on the east and WAN on the west. The Island has no railroad. Villages are scattered throughout the area and the population in 1940 was 18,000.

c. WATER SUPPLY

(1) OKINO DAITO JIMA. The best information available indicates the present water supply is dependent on catchments and shallow wells. Distillation units will therefore be needed in the early phases of occupation and wells driven to sea level in the center of the island will be the best source in the garrison phase.

(2) KUME SHIMA, like OKINO DAITO JIMA, apparently depends on catchments and wells for water supply. Distillation units and deeper wells will be required as at OKINO.

(3) MIYAKO JIMA has little or no surface water, but it is reported that deep wells will produce a large quantity of potable water. The enemy installations to supply his airfield development may be salvageable, but distilling units must be planned.

(4) KIKAI SHIMA's existing water installations are inadequate for our needs, practically all surface water being lost in permeable rock. Inland wells driven approximately to sea level and/or distillers will be required.

d. HARBORS

(1) OKINO DAITO SHIMA is surrounded by a narrow reef and has no protected inlet or anchorage. Small ships now approach the southwest side of the Island, making use of mooring buoys near a crane-equipped pier.

(2) KUME SHIMA has a useable harbor in SHIMAJIRI WAN, formed by coral reefs enclosing a large lagoon southeast of the Island. The anchorage has 15-20 fathoms and is well sheltered from all directions except southeast. Any size ship could enter, there being anchorage area for 4 cruisers and several destroyers, but local knowledge of the entrance shoals and of numerous dangers within the bay would be essential for further utilization. A channel breaks the reef at GIMA to afford

access to an anchorage suitable for small craft. Tidal currents cross-
ing the entrance, however, reach strengths of $3\frac{1}{2}$ knots.

(3) MIYAKO JIMA is surrounded by a coral reef. Northwest of the island
this formation protects MIYAKO HAKUCHI, an anchorage sufficient for
several capital ships plus attendant cruisers and destroyers, sheltered from all but northwest winds. Numerous detached patches of coral, some invisible, are present, but dangers from currents are negli-
gible. To the south of MIYAKO HAKUCHI, near the town of HIRARA, are
two smaller, deep water anchorages more sheltered but with narrow en-
trances. The port of HIRARA is approached by waters too shallow,
however, for any vessels other than small craft. JUNK BAY, south of
HIRARA, is too shallow for use as an anchorage but will accommodate
small landing craft. A secondary anchorage is possible on the east
coast, north of YASHIKUBARA. Although small and exposed to northwest
winds protection is otherwise adequate and water depth is sufficient
for any vessel. A small bay east of KURUMA JIMA has possibilities
of ten 600 yard berths in 10 to 20 fathoms of water. This site is
only one mile from an existing airfield.

(4) KIKAI JIMA's best harbor, SOMACHI HAKUCHI, a double inlet at the town
of SOMACHI, is small and open to winds between east and southeast,
but appears to be suitable for LSTs and like vessels. WAN MINATO,
on the southwest coast, almost dries and is available only to very
light craft. The waterfront at ONOTSU appears in photographs to be
of rough volcanic rock, but a small pier there may be salvageable.
A number of minor indentations afford passage through the reef for
small boats only.

e. BEACH CAPACITIES

(1) OKINO DAITO JIMA has no beaches, the only practicable landing point
being the phosphate pier and the adjoining seawall. This pier and
the small crane mounted thereon may survive the assault to be of use
in increasing the discharge capacity, but an estimate of 500 M/T per
day, adequate for expected needs, is all that is warranted by intelli-

- 109 -

gence information now available.

(2) KUME SHIMA has no known cargo handling facilities and all initial
discharge will have to be made over the beaches. GIMA KO is satisfactory for small craft and there is nearly 6,000 feet of shallow
water approaches or sandy beaches in this area. Because of limitations of exit from these beaches, tide conditions and relative expos-
ure, however, estimates of the capacity are below those experienced
in previous operations and vary widely. 500 M/T per day is a conservative figure subject to revision in view of later photographic coverage of the area.

SHIMAJIRI WAN offers greater capacity, at least 1700 M/T per day.
Possible landing sites along the southeast coast of the island total
6,600 feet of shallow water approach or sandy beach. Because of the
same limitations mentioned above for GIMA KO, however, the capacity
estimate is conservative and subject to revision by later intelligence
data. 2,200 M/T per day is insufficient for all anticipated needs,
but by landing the prescribed build-up supplies on OKINAWA and by
transshipment KUME's beach capacity becomes more nearly adequate.

(3) MIYAKO JIMA also is without any known cargo handling facilities, but
in view of the enemy's airfield development it is probable that some
improvements have been made. Considerable anchorage area is available favorably located off the best beaches, those on the western
coast. These may be used during any of the usual weather but use of
more exposed beaches on the southern and eastern coasts simultaneously
will be rarely if ever practicable. Capacities are conservatively
estimated as follows:

East Coast	1700 M/T per day, or
South Coast	1700 M/T per day.
West Coast	5100 M/T per day.
Total	6800 M/T per day.

This total is sufficient to handle tonnages planned for discharge.

(4) KIKAI JIMA's beach capacity appears to be far below anticipated requirements. Further intelligence may permit upward revision, but

current estimates are 500 M/T per day at SOMACHI HAKUCHI and an additional 500 for all of the island's other practicable landings. Limitations arising from off-shore conditions, lack of inlets and steep shores indicate little possibility of developing much greater capacity. Unless later photo coverage shows more favorable beaches the seizure and development of KIKAI SHIMA as proposed will be logistically feasible only by extensive use of exposed anchorages, small boats, cargo planes or gliders, parachute drops, or other relatively inefficient support methods of this nature.

4. TROOP AND TONNAGE REQUIREMENTS

   a. In setting up the troop lift and tonnage requirements, the following assumptions are made:

   (1) ESTIMATED TONNAGE LIFT PER MAN

	Total Lift	Orig. Equip. Initial Maint. & Const. Material	
		Initial Lift	Later Echelon
Tactical Troops - withdrawn	3 MT	3 MT	0
Tactical Troops - Remaining as part of garrison	5 MT	3 MT	2 MT
Garrison Troops - loaded with assault Forces	10 MT	3 MT	7 MT
Other Garrison Troops	10 MT	5 (Minimum)	5 MT

   (2) LOADING CAPACITIES WITHOUT STOWAGE

   AP's - 1500 Personnel and 200 MT

   AK's - 6500 MT for vessels scheduled to arrive during combat period (assumed 1st month), and 9000 MT for remainder.

b. OKINO DAITO JIMA

ESTIMATED PERSONNEL LIFT	1st Month	2nd Month	3rd Month	4th Month	5th Month	6th Month	7th Month	TOTAL
Tactical Troops	7319							7319
Garrison Troops	2000	925						2925
Replacements (not incl. Population)		640						640
TOTAL TROOPS	9319	1565						10662
In Assault Shipping	7819							7819
In Garrison Shipping	1500	1565						3065
AP's Required	1	1			(@ 1500 per AP)			2

POPULATION ESTIMATE

	1st Month	2nd Month	3rd Month	4th Month	5th Month	6th Month	7th Month	TOTAL
Balance forward	9319	9319						
Total Troops from "A"		925		(Less Replacements)				10244
SUB-TOTAL	9319	10244						10244
Withdrawals		6623						6623
Estimated Population	9319	3621	* 3621	3621	3621	3621	3621	6623

ESTIMATED DISCHARGE

| Capabilities in M/T's | 15000. | 15000 | 15000 | 15000 | 15000 | 15000 | 15000 | |

(Based on very meager information)

ESTIMATE OF TOTAL M/T of Original
Equipment & Initial Maintenance

Tactical Troops	@ 3 M/T per Man		6623 X 3 =					19869
	@ 5 M/T per Man		696 X 5 =					3480
Garrison Troops	@10 M/T per Man		2925 X 10 =					29250
								52599

- 112 -

ESTIMATE OF TONNAGE LIFT (M/T)

	1st Month	2nd Month	3rd Month	4th Month	5th Month	6th Month	7th Month	TOTAL
Maintenance @ .8 M/T per Man	7455	2890	2890	2582	2582	2582	2582	(52599
Build up Supply Level		2000	2000	1794				
Military Gov't (NONE)								
Tactical Troops in Assault Shipping	23457							23457
M/T for Garrison Lift	7500	10110	10110	1422				5794
	38412	15000	15000	5798	2582	2582	2582	
Lifted in Assault Shipping	23457							23457
Lifted in Garrison AP	2000	2000						
Lifted in AK	12955	13000	15000	5798	2582	(@ 2000 MT) 2582	2582	
AK's Required	2	2	2	1	1	0		
AK's Involved (120 Day Turn Around)	2	4	6	7	6	4	2	4000

* Used as basis for Supply Level

c. **NUME SHIMA**

ESTIMATED PERSONNEL LIFT

	1st Month	2nd Month	3rd Month	4th Month	5th Month	6th Month	7th Month	TOTAL
Tactical Troops	25736							25736
Garrison Troops	10000	19740						29740
Replacements (not incl. in Population)		1700	3000					4700
TOTAL TROOPS	35736	21440	3000					60176
In Assault Shipping	29736							29736
In Garrison Shipping	6000	21440	3000					30440
AP's Required	4	14	2					20

POPULATION ESTIMATE

	1st Month	2nd Month	3rd Month	4th Month	5th Month	6th Month	7th Month	TOTAL
Balance forward		35736						
Total Troops from "A"		19740			(Less Replacements)			
SUB-TOTAL	35736	55476						55476
Withdrawals		22644					22644	
Estimated Population	35736	32832	* 32832	32832	32832	32832	32832	

(@ 1500 per AP)

ESTIMATED DISCHARGE CAPABILITIES IN M/T

	1st Month	2nd Month	3rd Month	4th Month	5th Month	6th Month	7th Month
	66000	66000	66000	66000	66000	66000	66000 (Based on very meager information)

ESTIMATE OF TOTAL M/T OF ORIGINAL EQUIPMENT & INITIAL MAINTENANCE

Tactical Troops	(@ 3 M/T Per Men)	22644 X 3 = 67932
Garrison Troops	(@ 5 M/T Per Man)	3092 X 5 = 15460
	(@ 10 M/T Per Men)	29740 X 10 = 297400
		380792

- 114 -

ESTIMATE OF TONNAGE LIFT (M/T)

	1st Month	2nd Month	3rd Month	4th Month	5th Month	6th Month	7th Month	TOTAL
Maintenance @ .8 MT Per Man	28589	26265	26265	26265	26265	26265	26265	
Build Up Supply Level		17510	17510	17510				43902
Military Gov't.	300	300	300	300	300			
Tactical Troop Forces in Assault Shipping	89208							
MT for Garrison Lift	60000	57941	57941	57941	57941			(380972
Total For Ships**	88889	102016	102016	102016	84506	26265	26265	
Total For Discharge Capacity	178097	84506	84506	84506	84506	26265	26265	
Lifted in Assault Shipping	89208							89208
Lifted in Garrison AP	8000	28000	4000					40000
Lifted in AK	80889	74016	98016	102016	84506	26265	26265	
AK Required	12	8	11	11	9	3	3	
AK's Involved (120 day Turn Around)	12	20	31	42	39	34	26	

* Used as basis for supply level.

** Used in computing AK's required; Build-up Supply tonnages are planned to be landed on OKINAWA since KUME's beach capacity is apparently insufficient.

- 115 -

d. MIYAKO JIMA

ESTIMATED PERSONNEL LIFT

	1st Month	2nd Month	3rd Month	4th Month	5th Month	6th Month	7th Month	TOTAL
Tactical Troops	86646							86646
Garrison Troops	10000	29733	9366					49099
Replacements (not incl. Population)		3000	3000	3600				9600
TOTAL TROOPS	96646	32733	12366	3600				145345
In Assault Shipping	91646							91646
In Garrison Shipping	5000	32733	12366	3600				53699
AP's Required	3	22	8	2				35

POPULATION ESTIMATE

	1st Month	2nd Month	3rd Month	4th Month	5th Month	6th Month	7th Month	TOTAL
Balance Forward		96646	69548					
Total Troops from "A"	96646	29733	9366		(less Replacements)			135745
SUB-TOTAL	96646	126379	78914	78914	78914	78914	78914	
Withdrawals		56831						56831
Estimated Population	96646	69548	78914*	78914	78914	78914	78914	

ESTIMATED DISCHARGE CAPABILITIES IN M/T'S

	1st Month	2nd Month	3rd Month	4th Month	5th Month	6th Month	7th Month	TOTAL
	204000	204000	204000	204000	204000	204000	204000	204000 (Based on very meager information)

ESTIMATE OF TOTAL M/T OF ORIGINAL EQUIPMENT & INITIAL MAINTENANCE

Tactical Troops	@ 3 M/T per man	56831 X 3 =	170493
Garrison Troops	@ 5 M/T per man	29815 X 5 =	149075
	@10 M/T per man	49099 X 10 =	490990
			810558

ESTIMATE OF TONNAGE LIFT (M/T)

	1st Month	2nd Month	3rd Month	4th Month	5th Month	6th Month	7th Month	TOTAL
Maintenance @ .8 M/T per man	77317	55638	63131	63131	63131	63131	63131	
Build up Supply Level		30000	30000	30000	13236			103236
Military Gov't.		1500	1500	1500	1500	1500		
Tactical Troops in Assault Shipping.	274938							274938
M/T for Garrison Lift	50000	116862	109369	109369	126133	23887		(810558)
TOTAL	402255	204000	204000	204000	204000	88518	51618	
Lifted in Assault Shipping	274938							274938
Lifted in Garrison APs	6000	44000	16000	4000				
Lifted in AK	121317	160000	188000	200000	204000	88518 (@ 2000 MT)	63131	
AK's Required	19	18	21	23	23	10	7	
AK's Involved (120 Day Turn Around)	19	37	58	81	85	77	63	

* Used as basis for Supply Level.

e. ▮▮▮▮ T

KIKAI JIMA

ESTIMATED PERSONNEL LIFT

	1st Month	2nd Month	3rd Month	4th Month	5th Month	6th Month	7th Month	TOTAL
Tactical Troops	28374							28374
Garrison Troops	10000	20000	12325					42325
Replacements (not add'l. Population)		2500	1500			1500		5500
TOTAL TROOPS	38374	22500	13825			1500		76199
In Assault Shipping and by Parachute	33374							33374
In Garrison Shipping	5000	22500	13825					42825
AP's Required	3	15	9			1 (@ 1500 per AP)		28

POPULATION ESTIMATE

	1st Month	2nd Month	3rd Month	4th Month	5th Month	6th Month	7th Month	TOTAL
Balance Forward		38374	33134	45459	45459	45459	45459	
Total Troops to be Landed	38374	20000	12325					70699
SUB-TOTAL	38374	58374	45459		(less Replacements)			
Withdrawals		25240						252240
Estimated Population	38374	33134	45459*	45459	45459	45459	45459	25240

ESTIMATED DISCHARGE CAPABILITIES IN M/T.

	1st Month	2nd Month	3rd Month	4th Month	5th Month	6th Month	7th Month
	30000	30000	30000	30000	30000	30000	30000 (Based on very meager information)

ESTIMATE OF TOTAL M/T OF ORIGINAL EQUIPMENT & INITIAL MAINTENANCE

Tactical Troops	@ 3 M/T per man	28374 X 3 =	85122
Garrison Troops	@ 5 M/T per man	3134 X 5 =	15670
	@ 10 M/T per man	42325 X 10 =	423250
			524042

ESTIMATE OF TONNAGE LIFT (M/T)

	1st Month	2nd Month	3rd Month	4th Month	5th Month	6th Month	7th Month	TOTAL
Maintenance @ .8 M/T per man	30700	26507	36367	36367	36367	36367	36367	
Build up Supply Level **		12549	12000	12000	12000			
Military Gov't.		450	450	450	450			
Tactical Troops in Assault Shipping	100122							
M/T for Garrison Lift	20000	80784	80784	80784	80784	80784		
TOTAL (For Ships **		120290	129601	129601	129601	117151	36367	(524042
(less Build-up)		(12549)	(12000)	(12000)	(12000)			
(For Unloading Capacity	150822	107741	117601	117601	117601	117151	36367	
Lifted in Assault Shipping	100122							
Lifted in Garrison AP	6000	30000	18000			2000		
Lifted in AK	60851	90290	111601	129601	129601	115154	36367	
AK's Required	9	10	12	15	14	13	4	
AK's Involved (120 Day Turn Around)	9	19	31	46	51	54	46	

* Used as basis for supply level.

** Used in computing AK's required; Build-up Supply tonnages are planned to be landed on OKINAWA since KIKAI JIMA's beach capacity is inadequate.

5.   CONTEMPLATED DEVELOPMENT

a.   AIRFIELD DEVELOPMENT

(1) OKINO DAITO JIMA is too small for even a fighter strip in the prevailing wind direction and none is planned.

(2) KUME SHIMA has only one area suitable for dispersed airfields, the western tip of the island. Information is fragmentary but indicates that only two parallel fighter strips about 4500 feet long and 1000 feet apart can be accommodated, as shown on Supplement 3 to this Annex. Coral is available for surfacing. Solid rock and the topography appear to render the amount of grading to construct bomber fields prohibitive. If subsequent photo coverage confirms the unavailability of a VLR airfield site selection of another objective for this purpose is to be expected. For planning purposes logistic support of the alternate objective may be assumed to be the equivalent of that for KUME.

(3) MIYAKO JIMA has been described as "ideal" for airfields. Its flat surface appears to offer 6 or 7 possible sites for 7,000 foot fields. On 10 October 1944 three fields existed with a total of six runways, four having lengths of 4,000 to 5,500 feet. Both approach conditions and grading possibilities are favorable to further construction. As shown in Supplement 4 to this Annex development is contemplated as follows:

Four 7,000 foot strips, one per VLR Group, arranged in pairs.

Two fighter fields totalling three 5,000 foot strips, one field per Fighter Group plus one VF(N) or VMTB squadron.

Further intelligence may later dictate another arrangement but the above is considered a conservative estimate of the island's potentialities.

(4) KIKAI JIMA is known to have one existing airfield, approximately 4500 feet long, situated near WAN. As shown on Supplement 5 to Annex 2 of Appendix H the island's coastal plains offer the best additional sites and four fighter fields are contemplated. The terrain is

satisfactory and coral is readily obtainable for surfacing. Cross-drainage from inland slopes, particularly on the eastern coast sites, is expected to be the greatest problem. Several small villages will have to be removed complicating somewhat the care of civilians.

b. NAVAL FACILITIES

(1) At OKINO DAITO JIMA no naval facilities other than a GROPAC and a LORAN station are planned. Detailed composition of the GROPAC, to have 192 personnel, is given in Supplement 1 to Annex 3 of Appendix H; its principal components are Administration, Boat Pool, Surface Radar and Boat Repair units.

(2) KUME SHIMA's anchorage, SHIMAJIRI WAN, although relatively small warrants development and support. The components of this development, principally a standard GROPAC, a Boat Pool, a Harbor Entrance Control Post and allied harbor protection units are listed in Supplement 2 to Annex 3 of Appendix H. The aggregate personnel complement of the Naval Base will be 704.

(3) MIYAKO JIMA also has an anchorage worthy of development, and installation of an 848-man naval base consisting of forty-two components plus a 600-man boat pool is contemplated. The forty-two components, largest of which are the Port Director, Supply and Dispensary units, are listed in Supplement 3 to Annex 3 of Appendix H.

(4) KIKAI SHIMA will be the site of a GROPAC, to serve the small harbor at SOMACHI, and two PT Operating Bases. Twenty-six components, listed in Supplement 4 to Annex 3 of Appendix H, make up the 459-man GROPAC. Use of a 300-man Boat Pool is also contemplated.

c. HARBOR DEVELOPMENT AND WATERFRONT FACILITIES

(1) OKINO DAITO JIMA. Reconstruction of the phosphate loading pier and moorings will probably require augmentation by some device such as shore ramps and the use of LSTs to supply this island adequately. Lack of protected waters renders the use of pontoon piers doubtful.

No nets or underwater detection devices are considered necessary if the contemplated surface search radar can be augmented by anti-submarine craft. A GROPAC will provide essential waterfront services.

(2) KUME SHIMA. Although the initial assault on this Island will utilize GIMA KO, the limited potentialities of this harbor warrant only minor development as compared to SHIMAJIRI WAN to the southeast. A very narrow embayment in the coral of GIMA KO affords deep water as far as HANA SAKI, but the construction of wharves would be required to accommodate efficiently any but light craft. For use of GIMA KO as only a light craft anchorage no fixed underwater detection gear is contemplated. A slip mooring for a patrol vessel, however, will be required off the harbor entrance so that the patrol craft may use its detection gear free of engine noises while retaining a good position for interception.

SHIMAJIRI WAN is better suited for large ship discharge and is considered adequate for the island's needs. Should any major installation be added to the two fighter strips, however, clearing of the numerous coral heads in the bay will be necessary. For harbor protection the following is contemplated:

> Torpedo net from TOKUSHIMA BISE to HANAREGAA BISE, with tug operated gate.

> Sonobuoys on an arc 2 miles distant from the entrance, later supplemented by a herald southeast of HANAREGAA BISE.

> A Harbor Entrance Control Post with underwater detection station and surface search radar on SHIMAJIRI SAKI.

These positions are shown on Supplement 3 to Annex 2 of Appendix H.

Waterfront facilities will be provided by a GROPAC. Pontoon piers will be installed for discharge of small craft but wharfage for AK type vessels does not appear feasible.

(3) MIYAKO JIMA. Development of MIYAKO HAKUCHI into an anchorage affording the equivalent of 32 berths of 600 yards each is contemplated. Off-shore installations, shown in Supplement 4 to Annex 2 of Appendix H, will include:

Torpedo nets and underwater detection devices, including sonobuoys and eventually hydrophones.

A Harbor Entrance Control Post located on YERABU JIMA or IKEMA JIMA.

A surface search radar at the above post.

Picket boats sufficient to maintain constant patrol in the narrow passages and shallow water south of the anchorage.

Larger craft (83 ft. type) to patrol the northern anchorage approaches.

Mooring buoys in the small anchorage area between HIRARA and SHIMO ZAKI.

Channel buoys and channel entrance range.

Shore facilities to serve the harbor will be included in a CUB at HIRARA, and the installation of pontoon piers there is contemplated.

Additional possibilities, awaiting confirmation by later intelligence data, include a tanker mooring in the bay east of HIRARA and a secondary anchorage for about ten ships east of KURUMA JIMA. Should weather conditions prove favorable these bays, although relatively exposed, will be enclosed by nets and utilized.

(4) KIKAI SHIMA. The harbor of SOMACHI HAKUCHI, roughly only 800 yards by 500 yards in area, is the only anchorage potentially useful. Three sets of bow and stern moorings for small vessels and six pontoon wharves will be the maximum practicable development. Use of the large roadstead anchorage outside the harbor will be necessary, requiring installation of torpedo nets arranged in baffles as shown

on Supplement 5 to Annex 2 of Appendix H. Gates for emergency exit must be incorporated in the net baffles. Considerable depths close off-shore render fixed underwater detection devices inadvisable; constant patrol by anti-submarine craft will be necessary. Harbor service facilities ashore will be provided by a GROPAC at SOMACHI.

d. REQUIREMENTS

PROJECT	TOTAL BATT MOS OPER'L. COMPLETION	TOTAL BATT MOS FINAL COMPLETION	CONST. TRPS. REQUIRED	CONST. DAYS TO PLACE IN OPER. STATUS	CONST. DAYS FOR FINAL COMPLETION	CONST. EQUIP. M/T	CONST. MATL. M/T
OKINO DAITO JIMA							
LORAN STA.			USCG Pers. 36		(Organic)	1000	200
GROPAC			1/4 NCB (Pl) 279	As landed	180	2240	10964
TOTALS			315			3240	11164
KUME SHIMA (For Tentative Planning Purposes only pending selection of new sites due to apparent inadequacy of KUME SHIMA).							
1 AIRFIELD (New) 2 VLR Groups (90 Planes) 2 Strips 7000'x150'	5.25	16.5	2 Eng.Avn.Bns 1610	75**	236	21300	17300*
1 AIRFIELD (New) 2 VF Groups 1-VF(N)SQD (234 Planes) 2 Strips 5000'x150'	1.7	7.4	1 Eng.Avn.Bn 805	50**	225	7700*	10570*
GROPAC ROADS			1/2 NCB (Pl) 558	As landed	180	448C	1C964*
Spec. Const. Equip. Crushers, Distributors, etc.			Eng.Const.Bn 944		180	720C	556
TOTALS			3917	3 Eng.Avn.Bns 1/2 NCB (Pl) 1 Eng.Const.Bn		40680	39390

* Includes tonnage for replacement huts for hospital wards and flight personnel.

** One strip ∕ 20% taxiways and hardstands and minimum facilities.

PROJECT	TOTAL BATT MOS OPER'L. COMPLETION	TOTAL BATT MOS FINAL COMPLETION	CONST. TRPS. REQUIRED	CONST. DAYS TO PLACE IN OPER. STATUS	CONST. DAYS FOR FINAL COMPLETION	CONST. EQUIP. M/T (Organic)	CONST. MATL. M/T
MIYAKO JIMA							
AIRFIELD NO. 1 (Existing)	4.6	16.5	3 Eng.Avn.Bns 2415	50**	162	23100	17300*
2 VLR Groups (90 Planes)							
2 Strips 7000'x200'							
1 New Strip							
1 Strip Rebuilt & Ext'd.							
AIRFIELD NO. 2 (Existing) (Activated 5 days after seizure)	1.5	4.8	1 Eng.Avn.Bn 805	45**	144	7700	7090*
1 VF Group–111 Planes							
1 VF(N) Sqd. 12 Planes							
2 Strips to be extended to 5000'x150'							
AIRFIELD NO. 3 (New)	1.7	4.8	1 Eng.Avn.Bn 805	50	142	7700*	7090*
1 VF Group–111 Planes							
1 VMTB Sqd. – 18 Planes							
1 Strip 5000'x150'							
AIRFIELD NO. 4 (Existing)	4.6	16.5	3 Eng.Avn.Bns 2415	50**	162	23100*	17300*
2 VLR Groups – 90 Planes							
2 Strips 7000'x200'							
1 New Strip							
1 Strip Rebuilt & Ext'd							
CUB			2 NCB (P1) 2230	As landed	180	17920	28800
Roads			Eng.Const.Bn 944		180	7200	3000
Spec. Const. Equip. Asphalt, Plant, Crushers, Pavers, Distributors							
TOTALS						86720	80580
							3005

* Includes tonnage for replacement huts for hospital wards and flight personnel.

** One strip + 20% taxiways and hardstands and minimum facilities.

- 126 -

PROJECT	TOTAL BATT. MOS OPER'L. COMPLETION	TOTAL BATT. MOS FINAL COMPLETION	CONST. TRPS. REQUIRED	CONST. DAYS TO PLACE IN OPER. STATUS	CONST. DAYS FOR FINAL COMPLETION	CONST. EQUIP. M/T (Organic)	CONST. MATL. M/T
KIKAI JIMA							
AIRFIELD NO. 1 (Under Const.) 1-VF Group-111 Planes 1-VF(N) Sqd-12 Planes Strip 4500'x150'	1.2	3.7	1 Eng. Avn. Bn 805	35**	110	7700	5800*
AIRFIELD NO. 2 (New) 1 VF Group-111 Planes Strip 5500'x150'	1.5	3.8	1 Eng. Avn. Bn 805	50**	115	7700	5300*
AIRFIELD NO. 3 (New) 1-VF Group-111 Planes 1-VF(N) Sqd.-12 Planes Strip 5500'	1.6	4.0	1 Eng. Avn. Bn. 805	50**	120	7700	5600*
AIRFIELD NO. 4 (New) 1-VF Group-111 Planes 1-VMTB Sqd-18 Planes Strip 5500'x150'	1.6	4.0	1 Eng. Avn. Bn 805	50**	120	7700	5600*
GROPAC			½NCB (Pl) 558	As landed.	180		10964*
ROADS			Eng.Const.Bn. 994		180	7200	
2 PT Bases	2.0	4.0	INCB (Pl) 1115	30	60	8960	10400
Special Const. Equip. Distributors (Asphalt)							100
TOTALS			5837			46960	43764
GRAND TOTAL (All Four (4) Locations)			19683			177600	174898

* Includes tonnage for replacement huts for hospital wards and flight personnel.

** One strip / 20% taxiways and hardstands and minimum facilities.

6. MEDICAL FACILITIES AND EVACUATION POLICY

a. ESTIMATE OF CASUALTIES

Type of Casualty	OKINO	KUME	MIYAKO	KIKAI
Dead and Missing	160	800	2400	1000
Local Hospitalization	150	800	2400	500
Requiring Evacuation	490	2400	7200	3500
Totals	800	4000	12000	5000

b. EVACUATION

(1) Casualties from OKINO will be evacuated directly to the MARIANAS, by surface only. An AH or APH will be provided for emergencies and evacuation. From all other objectives evacuation by surface is contemplated and by air when airfields are available, to the MARIANAS and OKINAWA. MIYAKO casualties will also be sent to the PHILIPPINES upon advance arrangement by Cincpoa with CinCSWPA. Bed credits required:

	OKINAWA	MARIANAS	PHILIPPINES
OKINO	-	490	-
KUME	1000*	1400	-
MIYAKO	500*	2000	4500
KIKAI	1000	2500	-
Totals	2500	6390	4500

* (Staging, enroute MARIANAS or PHILIPPINES).

(2) Surface ships required:

Objective	No. and Type Ship	Total Capacity
OKINO	1 AH or APH	500
KUME	2 AH	1000
	24 LST or 10 APA	1400
MIYAKO	4 AH*	4000
	3 APH	2100
	8 APA	1100
KIKAI	2 AH	1000
	3 APH	2100
	3 APA or 7 LST	400

* 2 Trips.

c. HOSPITALIZATION

In the assault phase at all objectives medical units of the assault force will provide hospitalization. Garrison hospitalization requirements will be as follows:

OKINO	150 beds.
KUME	1025 beds.
MIYAKO	3050 beds.
KIKAI*	1850 beds.

* With a 15-day evacuation policy.

d. CARE OF CIVILIANS

Objective	Estimated Casualties	Medical Service by
OKINO	150	Med. Units of Assault Force.
KUME	1300	Mil. Govt. Units - 100 beds.
MIYAKO	6000	Mil. Govt. Units - 600 beds.
KIKAI	1800	Mil. Govt. Units - 150 beds.

7. LOGISTIC SUPPORT FOR THE FLEET

In addition to the harbors to be utilized in Phases I and II, OKINAWA (NAKAGUSUKU WAN) will be available during Phase III for the services of fleet oilers, ammunition ships, supply ships and barges, and limited ship repair facilities. Ship repair facilities and emergency logistic replenishment will be available at MANUS and to a lesser extent at LEYTE, subject to arrangement by Cincpoa with CinCSWPA. Fleet fuel consumption is estimated as follows:

L $\neq$ 30 to L $\neq$ 60	4,200,000 bbls.
L $\neq$ 60 to L $\neq$ 90	4,200,000 bbls.
L $\neq$ 90 to L - 120	5,100,000 bbls.

In the event the British Pacific Fleet takes part in this operation fuel requirements will be increased by approximately 700,000 barrels for each of the above periods. All other aspects of logistic support for the Fleet for Phases I and II apply equally to Phase III.

8.   LOGISTIC SUPPORT OF LAND BASED FORCES

   a.   RESPONSIBILITY FOR SUPPLY

Forces in Phase III, mounted from areas other than OKINAWA, will be furnished initial supplies by Commanders responsible for furnishing such supplies to forces of Phase I. Forces mounting from OKINAWA will be furnished initial supplies by ComGenTENTHArmy within total quantities of supplies made available by Cincpoa. Commanders responsible for providing supplies subsequent to initial mounting for Phase I will be similarly responsible for resupply of Phase III forces.

   b.   SUPPLIES TO ACCOMPANY TROOPS

For the forces in Phase III mounting from points other than OKINAWA the same levels of initial supplies as prescribed for Phase I (page 46, paragraph 7 b., Appendix E) will be required. Supplies to accompany forces mounting from OKINAWA will be determined and provided by ComGenTENTH Army from total quantities of supplies made available to him by Cincpoa for all phases of the ICEBERG operation.

   c.   SUPPLY LEVELS TO BE ESTABLISHED AND MAINTAINED AT THE OBJECTIVE

Supply levels for Phase III will be as prescribed for Phase I. ComGenTENTH Army is authorized to distribute stocks among various islands to maintain the prescribed total and stock level.

   d.   RESERVE SUPPLIES

Since Phase III forces are largely redeployed from Phase I, the reserve levels and supplies (except Class III) established for Phase I will continue through Phase III.

Class III Reserves

(1) All products (less Avgas), drummed:

One ship will be loaded on West Coast with 30 days of Class III (less Avgas) supplies in drums as follows: (Approximately 30 days supply for 50,000 troops)(12 days approximately for all garrisons at all 4 targets).

		Greases in Pounds	
Mogas	17,000 Drums		
White Gas	4,000 "	2-107	17,500
Diesel	8,500 "	2-108	6,250

- 130 -

Kerosene	350 Drums	2-109	2,000
Avlube 1120	300 "	2-110	1,250
SAE 10 lube oil	50 "	Gear Lube	
SAE 30 lube oil	850 "	SAE 90	47,650
SAE 50 lube oil	150 "		

This ship to arrive at OKINAWA by L / 70 and to be held in reserve for Phase III on call of Commanding General 10th Army. If these supplies are not used sooner, they will be discharged at OKINAWA by L / 120 and constitute drummed reserves.

(2) Avgas and related Avlube, drummed:

Two shiploads (60,000 drums Avgas, 2000 Avlube) as provided for in Annex D to Cincpac-Cincpoa Operation Plan 14-44 (para. 5(d) 1, page 11), if not used in Phases I and II, or portions thereof not used, will be available to ComGen10thArmy on call.

(3) All products, bulk:

No AOGs in addition to those provided for Phases I and II are considered necessary for Phase III. However, ComServPac will have four additional YOGLs (all non self-propelled) available to ComGen10thArmy upon prior arrangement with ComServPac.

To reduce handling of drums to a minimum, AOGs are to be at targets, and installation of flexible pipelines, submarine lines and temporary bulk storage ashore near landing beaches, is to be commenced in initial assault, or as soon after assault as possible.

e. METHOD OF SUPPLY

(1) OKINC.

Essential maintenance supplies for 30 days of all classes (except Class III which will be 15 days and Class V) for all elements of the expeditionary troops employed in Phase IIIa will be provided by Com-Gen10thArmy on call of Commander Expeditionary Troops Phase IIIa and will constitute the first resupply shipment. These supplies will be loaded on the WEST COAST, will sail at such time as to arrive ENIWETOK by T-15 (L / 45) and will be loaded for optional discharge in one ship also carrying Phase I and/or Phase II maintenance supplies, to sail with one of the regular OKINAWA maintenance shipments. It will be

held at ENIWETOK for forward movement on call of ComGen10thArmy.
Subsequently, ComGen10thArmy will be responsible for the resupply
of the landing and garrison forces, utilizing stocks and vessels
available locally to him. The regular OKINAWA maintenance shipments
will include supplies necessary for the support of the OKINO Forces.
No bulk storage of Mogas and Diesel is considered necessary for this
island; all units stationed there will be supplied with Class III
products (less Aviation) in drums, trans-shipped from OKINAWA, with
special consideration to operative requirements of LORAN equipment.

(2) KUME JIMA.

Essential maintenance supplies for 30 days of all classes (except
Class III which will be 15 days, and Class V) for all elements of the
landing and garrison forces scheduled to be at the objective by K ∕ 35
(L ∕ 105) will be loaded on the WEST COAST and will sail at such
times so as to arrive at ENIWETOK at K - 15 (L ∕ 55). This shipment
will sail from the WEST COAST with one of the regular OKINAWA maintenance shipments, but will be loaded in separate ships. It will be
held at ENIWETOK for forward movement on call of ComGen10thArmy and
will constitute the first re-supply shipment for Phase IIIb.

The second and succeeding re-supply shipments will be scheduled to
arrive at ENIWETOK at 10-day intervals commencing K - 5 (L ∕ 65)
and accompanying regular OKINAWA maintenance shipments. These shipments will be held at ENIWETOK for forward movement on call of
ComGen10thArmy. Supplies for the second and third re-supply shipments, loaded in separate ships, will contain 15 days' supply of
all classes (except Class III Avgas and Class V) for all elements
of the landing and garrison forces to be supported. Supplies for
the fourth and succeeding re-supply shipments, loaded in separate
ships, will contain 15 days' supply of all classes (except drummed
Avgas, Mogas and Diesel; and Class V) for all elements of the landing and garrison forces to be supported. These shipments will continue until the prescribed area levels are reached; thereafter only
sufficient supplies will be included to maintain these area levels.

Assuming the VLR bomber field is operational by K $\neq$ 75 and a fighter field by K $\neq$ 50 Avgas requirements are estimated as follows:

K $\neq$ 45 -	K $\neq$ 60	629,000 gal. in bulk
K $\neq$ 61 -	K $\neq$ 90	5,195,000 gal. in bulk

These quantities and accompanying Avlubes will be delivered by ComServPac to the OKINAWA area prior to the respective periods shown, to be discharged as directed by ComGen10thArmy. It is anticipated a minimum of 20,000 bbls. Avgas storage will be available on this island by K $\neq$ 45. Re-supply shipments of Avgas will be made in bulk as prescribed for Phase I.

Re-supply of Class III products other than Avgas will consist of three (3) fifteen (15) day shipments in drums. Subsequent maintenance shipments will consist of approximately 15 days supplies (less Avgas, Mogas, and Diesel) until the prescribed levels are reached. Re-supply of Mogas and Diesel after the 3rd 15 day shipment will be in bulk; it is contemplated bulk storage for these products will be operative K $\neq$ 15.

(3) MIYAKO JIMA.

Essential maintenance supplies for 30 days of all classes (except Class III which will be 15 days; and Class V) for all elements of the landing and garrison forces scheduled to be at the objective by A $\neq$ 35 (L $\neq$ 125) will be loaded on the WEST COAST and sailed at such time or times so as to arrive at ENIWETOK at A - 15 (L $\neq$ 75).   This shipment will sail from the WEST COAST with one of the regular OKINAWA maintenance shipments, but will be loaded in separate ships. It will be held at ENIWETOK for forward movement on call of ComGen10thArmy and will constitute the first re-supply shipment for Phase IIIc.

The second and succeeding re-supply shipments will be scheduled to arrive at ENIWETOK at 10-day intervals commencing A - 5(L+85) and accompanying regular OKINAWA maintenance shipments. These shipments will be held at ENIWETOK for forward movement on call of ComGen10thArmy. Supplies for the second and third re-supply shipments, loaded in separate ships, will contain 15 days' supply of all classes (except Class III Avgas and Class V) for all elements of the landing and garrison forces to be supported. Supplies for the fourth and succeeding re-supply shipments, loaded in separate ships, will contain 15 days' supply of all classes (except drummed Avgas, Mogas and Diesel; and Class V) for all elements of the landing and garrison forces to be supported. These shipments will continue until the prescribed area levels are reached; thereafter only sufficient supplies will be included to maintain area levels.

Assuming the four airfields to be developed on this island are activated as scheduled Avgas requirements are estimated as follows:

A + 5 - A + 30	822,500 gals plus related avlubes
A +31 - A + 60	3,517,500 " " " "
A +61 - A + 90	8,579,000 " " " "

Of these quantities the first 25 days supply will be required in drums - 15,519 drums of Avgas and 465 drums (24,645 gals.) of Avlube. This drummed supply will be mounted with and will accompany the first Air Corps units to operate from the objective. Re-supply shipments of Avgas will be made in bulk as prescribed for Phase I.

Re-supply of Class III products other than Avgas will

consist of three (3) fifteen (15) day shipments in drums. Subsequent maintenance shipments will consist of approximately 15 days maintenance supplies (less Avgas, Mogas and Diesel), until the prescribed levels are reached. Thereafter, only sufficient supplies will be included to maintain those levels. Re-supply of Mogas and Diesel after the third 15-day shipment will be in bulk; it is contemplated bulk storage for these products will be operative by A $\not= $ 15.

(4) KIKAI JIMA.

Essential maintenance supplies for 30 days of all classes (except Class III which will be 15 days and Class V) for all elements of the landing and garrison forces scheduled to be at the objective by F $\not= $ 35 (L $\not= $ 155) will be loaded on the WEST COAST and sailed at such time or times so as to arrive at ENIWETOK at F - 15 (L $\not= $ 105). This shipment will sail from the WEST COAST with one of the regular OKINAWA maintenance shipments, but will be loaded in separate ships. It will be held at ENIWETOK for forward movement on call of ComGen10thArmy, and will constitute the first re-supply shipment for Phase IIId.

The second and succeeding re-supply shipments will be scheduled to arrive at ENIWETOK at 10-day intervals commencing F - 5 (L $\not= $ 115) and accompanying regular OKINAWA maintenance shipments. These shipments will be held at ENIWETOK for forward movement on call of ComGen10thArmy. Supplies for the second and third re-supply shipments, loaded in separate ships, will contain 15 days' supply of all classes (except Class III Avgas and Class V) for all elements of the landing and garrison forces to be supported. Supplies for the fourth and succeeding re-supply shipments, loaded in separate ships, will contain 15 days' supply of all classes (except drummed Avgas, Mogas and Diesel; and Class V) for all elements of the landing and garrison forces to be supported.

These shipments will continue until the prescribed area levels

are reached; thereafter, only sufficient supplies will
be included to maintain area levels.

Assuming the four airfields are activated on KIKAI JIMA as
scheduled Avgas requirements are estimated as follows:

$$\text{F} \not= 35 - \text{F} \not= 60 \qquad 1,776,800 \text{ gals. in bulk}$$
$$\text{F} \not= 61 - \text{F} \not= 90 \qquad 3,850,000 \text{ gals. in bulk}$$

These quantities and related Avlubes will be delivered
by ComServPac to the OKINAWA area prior to the respective
periods shown, to be discharged as directed by ComGen10thArmy.
It is anticipated a minimum of 20,000 bbls. Avgas storage
will be available on this island by F $\not=$ 35. Re-supply shipments of Avgas will be made in bulk as prescribed for Phase I.
Re-supply of Class III products other than Avgas will consist
of three (3) fifteen (15) day shipments in drums. Subsequent
maintenance shipments will consist of approximately 15 days
maintenance supplies (less Avgas, Mogas and Diesel), until the
prescribed levels are reached. Thereafter, only sufficient
supplies will be included to maintain those levels. Re-supply
of Mogas and Diesel after the third 15 day shipment will be in
bulk; it is contemplated bulk storage for these products will
be operative by F $\not=$ 15.

(5) Individual shipping designators will be assigned to KUME,
MIYAKO and KIKAI to facilitate these direct maintenance shipments.

9. MILITARY GOVERNMENT

Civilian requirements will be provided in the manner set forth in the
Logistic Measures for Phase I, utilizing additional Military Government
Teams as shown in the Troop List, Phase III.

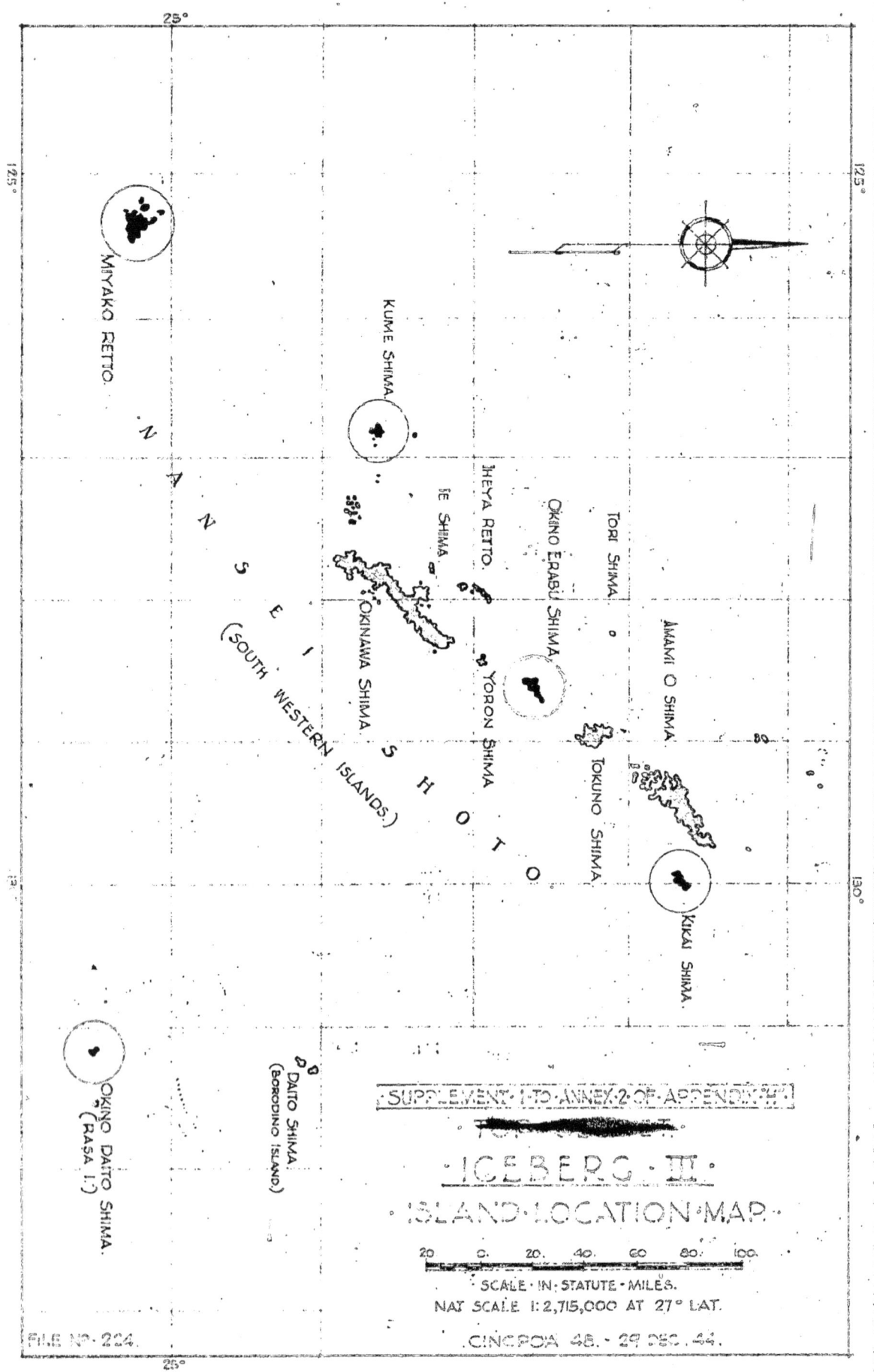

MIYAKO RETTO.

N A N S E I

KUME SHIMA.

(SOUTH WESTERN ISLANDS)

IE SHIMA.

IHEYA RETTO.

OKINO ERABU SHIMA.

TORI SHIMA.

AMAMI O SHIMA.

OKINAWA SHIMA.

YORON SHIMA.

S H O T O

TOKUNO SHIMA.

KIKAI SHIMA.

OKINO DAITO SHIMA.
(RASA I.)

DAITO SHIMA.
(BORODINO ISLAND)

SUPPLEMENT 1 TO ANNEX 2 OF APPENDIX

ICEBERG · III ·

ISLAND · LOCATION · MAP ·

20   0.   20.   40.   60   80   100.

SCALE · IN · STATUTE · MILES.

NAT SCALE 1:2,715,000 AT 27° LAT.

CINCPOA 48. - 29 DEC. 44.

FILE Nº 224.

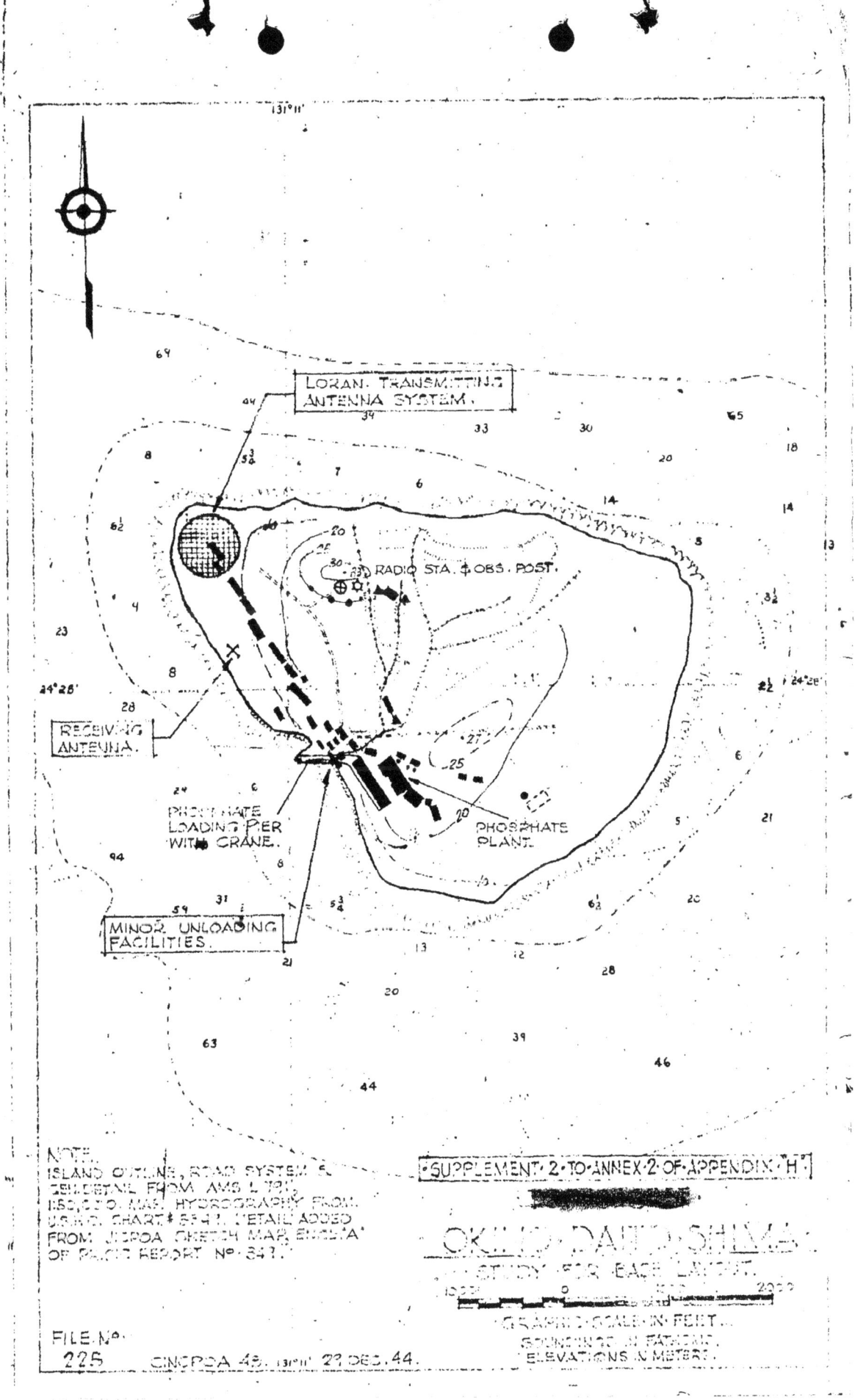

131°11'

LORAN. TRANSMITTING
ANTENNA SYSTEM.

RADIO STA. & OBS. POST.

RECEIVING
ANTENNA.

PHOSPHATE
LOADING PIER
WITH CRANE.

PHOSPHATE
PLANT.

24°28'

24°28'

MINOR UNLOADING
FACILITIES.

NOTE:
ISLAND OUTLINE, ROAD SYSTEM &
DETAIL FROM AMS L762.
ADDED TO AMS. HYDROGRAPHY FROM
U.S.H.O. CHART # 5541. DETAIL ADDED
FROM JICPOA SKETCH MAP EVELNA
OF PAINT REPORT No 347.

FILE No.
225   CINCPOA 49. 131°11' 23 DEC. 44.

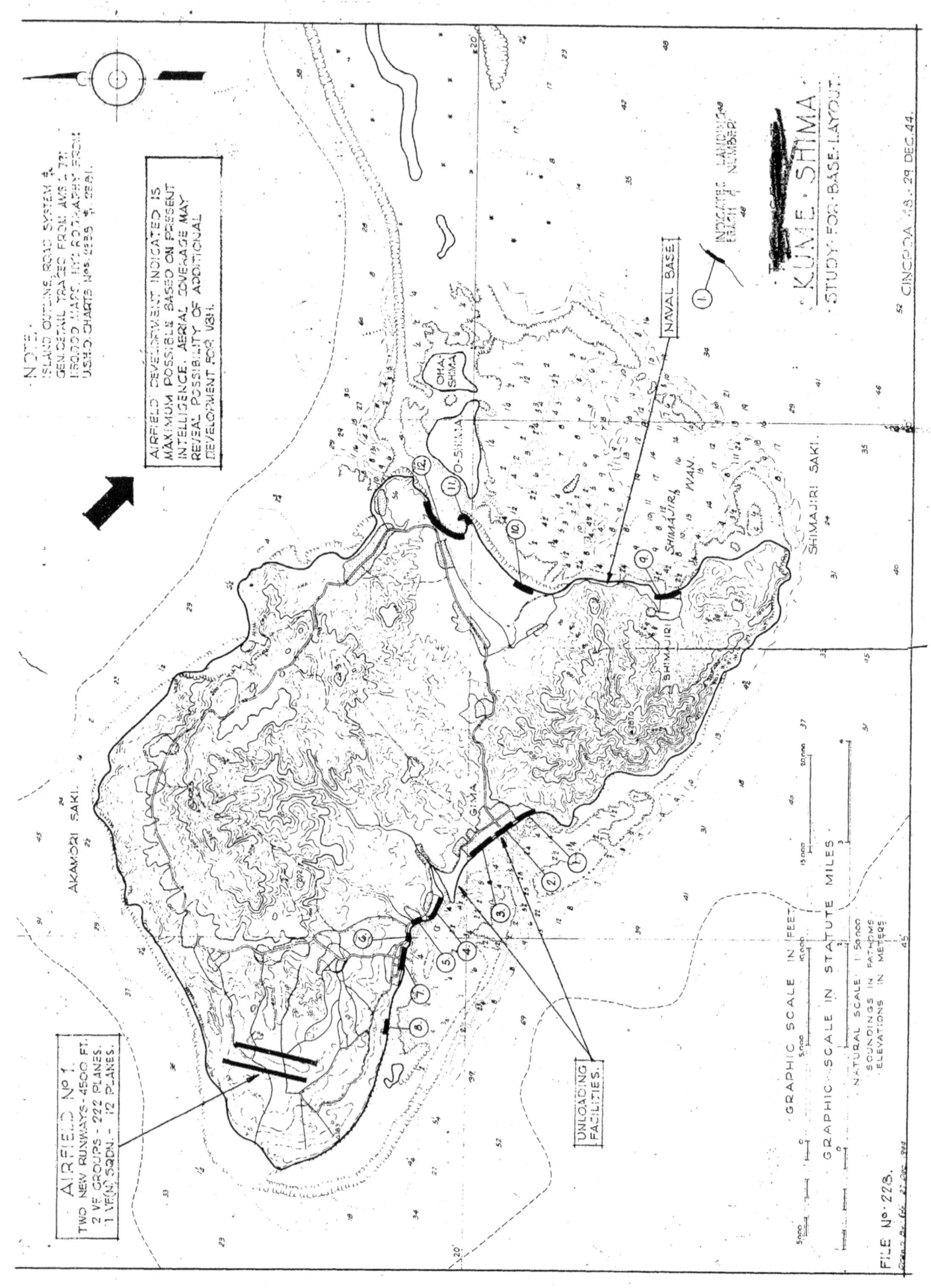

NOTE:
ISLAND OUTLINE ROAD SYSTEM &
GEN. DETAIL TRACED FROM AWS-72;
1:50,000 MAPS REPROGRAPHY FROM
U.S.H.O. CHARTS Nos. 6235 & 6234.

AIRFIELD DEVELOPMENT INDICATED IS
MAXIMUM POSSIBLE BASED ON PRESENT
INTELLIGENCE. AERIAL COVERAGE MAY
REVEAL POSSIBILITY OF ADDITIONAL
DEVELOPMENT FOR V8H.

AIRFIELD No. 1.
TWO NEW RUNWAYS - 4500 FT.
2 VF GROUPS - 222 PLANES.
1 VF(N) SQDN. - 12 PLANES.

UNLOADING FACILITIES.

NAVAL BASE

INDICATES LANDING
BEACH & NUMBER

KUME SHIMA.
STUDY FOR BASE LAYOUT.

CINCPOA 48. 29 DEC. 44.

OHA SHIMA

O-SHIMA

SHIMAJIRI WAN.

SHIMAJIRI

SHIMAJIRI SAKI.

GIMA

AKAMORI SAKI.

GRAPHIC SCALE IN FEET.

GRAPHIC SCALE IN STATUTE MILES.

NATURAL SCALE 1:50,000
SOUNDINGS IN FATHOMS
ELEVATIONS IN METERS

FILE No. 223.

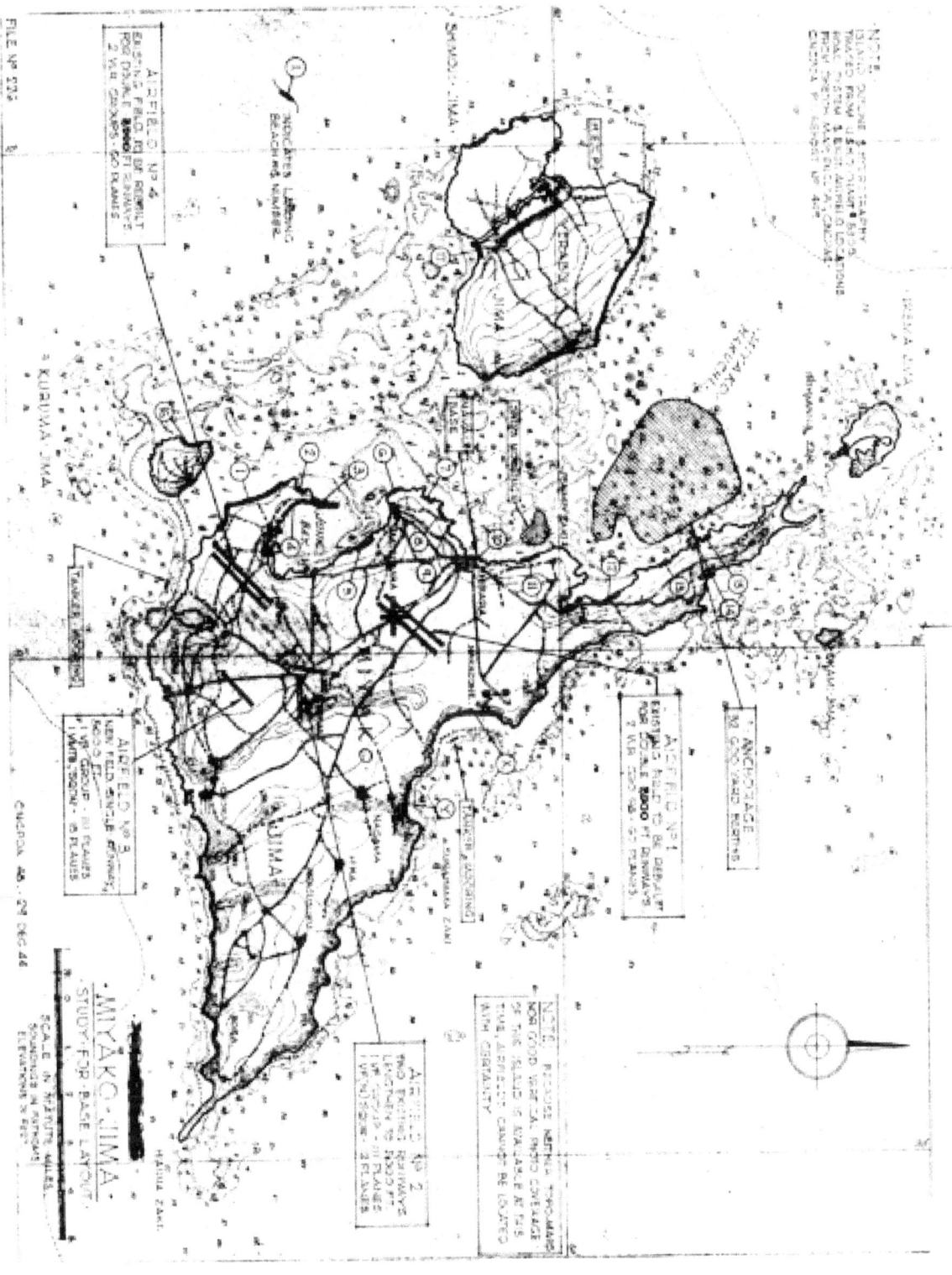

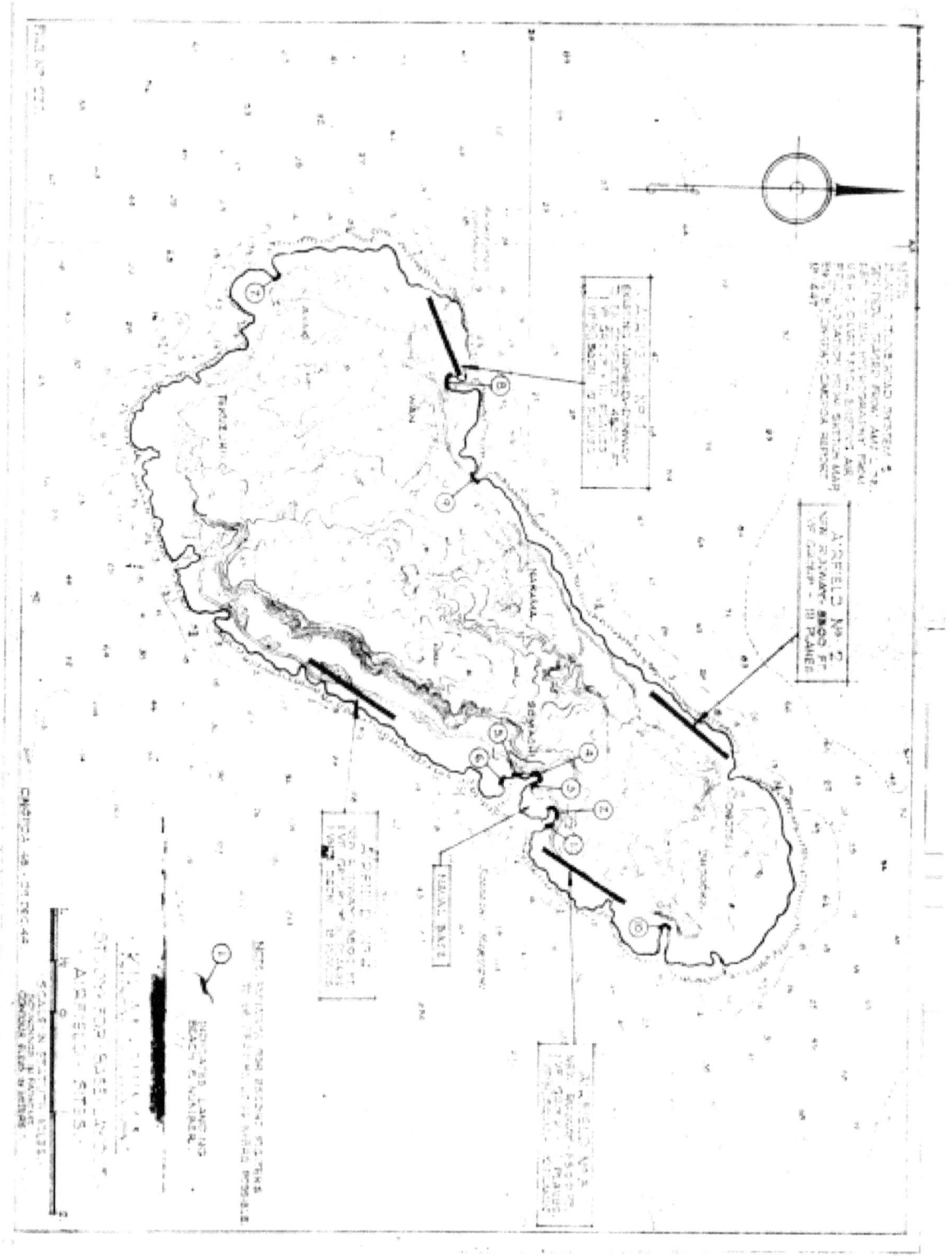

CHECK LIST OF PRINTING INTELLIGENCE

Island	Hydrographic Office Chart No.	Army Map Service Map No.	Strategic Engineering Study No. 119 (C of E., U.S.A.) Volume and Page	ONI 60 Information Bulletin Page	Cincpac-Cincpoa Reconnaissance Photos Jicpoa No.	Photographic Intelligence Reports
Kikai	US H.O. #5304	AMS L751 Sheet #20	II: 238,239,270,251,334, 335,372,404,405	197,198, "Amami Gunto" Bull. No.163-44, pp. 22-28	7534-2,7535-2, 7536-2,7537-3, 7538-3	Cincpac-poa No. 447 (map)
Kume	US H.O. #2581 #2338	AMS L751 Sheets 54, 55,60	I: 22,23,24,25,28,27,66,67, 68,69,70,71,100,101,120, 121,122,123,124,125,156, 158,160,192,193,194,195, 196,197	106,109, "Okinawa Gunto" Bull.7752-1,7561-46, 110 (map) No. 161-44 pt 58-61 12020-2		Cincpac-poa Nos. 450,451
Miyako	US H.O. #5308 #1940	None AMS L751	I: 20,21,64,55,118,119,154, 190,191	21,72,75, "Sakishima Gunto" 76,77 (map) Bull. No. 152-44 pp. 25-36	7674-1,7655-1, 7676-1,7677-2, 7678-2,7679-2, 7680-3,7682.5, 7683-5,11323-6, 11324-6,11325-6, 11326-7,11327-8, 11328-8,11934-9, 11935-10,11936-11, 12021-12	Cincpac-poa Nos. 450,451
Okino Daito	US H.O. #5340	Sheet #69 AMS L701	I: 44,45,86,140,141,176,212, 213	95,96, "Nansei Shoto" Bull. No. 63-44, pp. 21	6959-1,7655-3, 11329-4,11331-6, 11332-6,11330-5, 12025-7	Prisic #349/ Hq. Comdr. Shore Based AP, Forward Area, Cent.Pac.P.I. Memo No. 47/ Interpron 2 No.219

NOTE: The "Revised Estimate of Nansei Shoto" by the Joint Intelligence Study Publishing Board, Washington, 1 August 1944, contains maps and other pertinent material.

File No. 262

ICEBERG PHASE III

ANNEX 3 TO APPENDIX H

TROOP LIST

S U M M A R Y   O F   P E R S O N N E L

ASSAULT FORCES

(a) Total 148,075

(b) To be used in Garrison Force 36,737

(c) To be withdrawn 111,338

GARRISON FORCES

(a) To be moved to area after assault .. 123,997

(b) To be provided by Assault Force 36,737

(c) Total 160,734

THIS LIST OF ASSAULT AND SUPPORTING SERVICE TROOPS IS DEEMED THE MINIMUM FOR ACCOMPLISHMENT OF PHASE III OF THIS OPERATION. UNITS TO BE REDEPLOYED FROM PHASE I ARE SO INDICATED, BUT AVAILABILITY OF OTHER UNITS HAS NOT BEEN DETERMINED. NOTE THE REPLACEMENT OF VBH UNITS BY VLR UNITS THROUGHOUT PHASE III.

ANNEX 3 TO APPENDIX H
SUMMARY — ICEBERG TROOP LIST — PHASE IIIa

OKINO DAITO JIMA

Units	ASSAULT				GARRISON				Differences Assault and Garrison	
	Army	Navy	Marine	Total	Army	Navy	Marine	Total	Decreases	Increases
COMBAT										
Headquarters			3218	3218	1070	49		1119	3218	1119
Battalions			295	295	445			445	295	445
A.A. Artillery			602	602	396			396	602	396
Artillery			346	346	30			30	346	30
Armored										
Chemical Warfare	136			136					136	
Total Combat	136		4461	4597	1941	49		1990	4597	1990
SERVICE										
Engineers		557	206	763	125	279		404		
Medical			204	204	110			110		
Ordnance			46	46						
Quartermaster			514	514	162			162		
Signal	158		167	325	229	35		264		
Military Police			26	26	44			44		
Adjutant General					9			9		
Transportation	219		585	804	219			219		
Naval Base Units		40		40		344		344		
Military Government						75		75		
Total Service	377	597	1748	2722	898	733		1631	2026	935
OKINO Total	513	597	6209	7319	2839	782		3621	6623	2925

Unit	T/O	ASSAULT			GARRISON			Remarks
		Army	Navy	Marine	Army	Navy	Marine	
IS COM HQ	A-3, N3A			1 3218	1 1070	1 49		
INFANTRY REGT	F-10							
INFANTRY BN (reinf)	7-15							
A.A. ARTILLERY								
AAA A/W Btry	B-172			1 295	1 150			
AAA Gun Btry	44-17				1 164			
AAA A/W Btry	44-127				1 91			Light AA Gp. AAA Bn
AAA S/L Plat	44-138				1 40			
HQ & HQ Det AAA Gun Bn	44-116							From Phase I
	Total			295	445			
ARTILLERY								
F.A. Bn (105 How)	F-25			1 602				
155 MM Gun (CA) Bn (- 1 Btry)	4-55				1 300			
F.A. Btry (105 MM)	6-27				1 96			
	Total			602	396			
ARMORED								
Med Tank Co	F-76			1 169				
LVT (A) Co	F-1016			1 177	1 30			
Med Tk Plat	17-27							
	Total			346	30			
CHEMICAL								
Chemical (MTZD) Co	3-27	1 136						
	Total	136						

Unit	T/O	ASSAULT			GARRISON			Remarks
		Army	Navy	Marine	Army	Navy	Marine	
ENGINEER								
Naval C Bn	P-1		1/2 557			1/4 279		From Phase I
Pioneer Co	F-36			1 206				From Phase I
Total			557	206		279		
MEDICAL								
Medical Co	F-51			2 204				
Sta Hosp (150)	8-560				1 100			
Malaria Control Unit					1 12			
Malaria Survey Unit					1 13			
Total				204	125			
ORDNANCE								
Ordnance Maint Plat	F-61			1 35				
Tank Maint Sec	F-61			1 11				
Ord Lt M Co	9-8				1 110			
Total				46	110			
QUARTERMASTER								
Supply and Service Plat	F-62			1 114				
Det Mar Fld Dep	E-770			1 400				
QM Comp Co	10-500				1 162			From Phase I
Total				514	162			
SIGNAL								
JASCO Det	E-518			1/3 167	1 121			
Det Sig Serv Co	11-500	1 62			1 96			
Sig Constr Plat	11-67	1 96			1 12			
Navy Comm Unit	-					1 35		
Radar Maint Det	11-167							
Total		158		267	229	35		

Unit	T/O	ASSAULT			GARRISON			Remarks
		Army	Navy	Marine	Army	Navy	Marine	
MILITARY POLICE								
M.P. Plat	F-90							
M.P. Plat ZI	19-57				1 44			
Total				26				
ADJUTANT-GENERAL								
Army Postal Unit Type B	12-605				1 3			
Gar Censor	-				1 6			
Total					9			
TRANSPORTATION								
Motor Transport Co	F-56			1 115				
Amph Trac Co	F-1015			2 284				
Amph Trk Co	E-705			1 186				
Port Co	55-117	219			1 219			
Total		219		585	219			
NAVAL								
GROPAC	-					1 192		Includes Boat Pool (See attached schedule)
Loran Station	-					1 63		After construction reduced to 35.
Garrison Beach Party	-					89		
Total						344		
CIVIL AFFAIRS								
Mil Govt A Det	-		1 14			1 14		
Mil Govt B Det	-		1 26			1 26		
Mil Govt Civ Camp Orgn	-					1 35		
Total			40			75		
TOTALS	-	513	597	6209	2839	782		
GRAND TOTAL ALL SERVICES		ASSAULT - 7319			GARRISON - 3621			

ANNEX 3 TO APPENDIX "H"

SUMMARY - ICEBERG TROOP LIST - PHASE IIIb

KUME SHIMA

Units	ASSAULT				GARRISON				Differences Assault and Garrison	
	Army	Navy	Marine	Total	Army	Navy	Marine	Total	Decreases	Increases
COMBAT										
Headquarters	--	--	--	--	505	35	--	540	--	540
Divisions	14063	--	--	14063	3206	--	--	3206	14063	3206
Aviation	--	--	--	--	6448	--	--	6448	--	6448
AA Artillery	801	--	--	801	3043	--	--	3043	801	3043
Artillery	--	--	--	--	970	--	--	970	--	970
Armored	1472	--	--	1472	117	--	--	117	1472	117
Chemical Warfare	596	--	--	596	--	--	--	--	596	--
Total Combat	16932	--	--	16932	14289	35	--	14324	16932	14324
SERVICE										
Signal	845	--	--	845	678	66	--	744	652	551
Chemical	--	--	--	--	18	--	--	18	--	18
Aviation	159	--	--	159	5194	--	--	5194	--	5035
Medical	399	87	--	486	1149	101	--	1250	376	1140
Ordnance	935	--	--	935	827	--	--	827	388	280
Engineer	2769	--	--	2769	5865	558	--	6423	2769	6423
Naval Base Units	--	89	--	89	--	793	--	793	704	--
Transportation	1835	--	--	1835	471	--	--	471	1364	--
Military Police	507	--	--	507	344	--	--	344	163	--
Quartermaster	1137	--	--	1137	1688	--	--	1688	--	551
Adjutant General	--	--	--	--	74	--	--	74	--	74
Military Government	--	42	--	42	--	92	--	92	--	50
Total Service	8586	218	--	8804	16308	1610	--	17918	5712	14826
KUME TOTAL	25518	218	--	25736	30597	1645	--	32242	22544	29150

Unit	T/O	ASSAULT Army	ASSAULT Navy	ASSAULT Marine	GARRISON Army	GARRISON Navy	GARRISON Marine	Remarks
CIC DET	30-500				2 25			From Phase I
IS COM HQ	Total				1 480	35		From Phase I
					505	35		
AMPHIB. DIVISION	7-	1 4,032						
INFANTRY REGT	7-11	31						
G-2 TEAMS	Total	1 4,063		1	1 3206			
					3206			
AIR FORCES								
VF Grp Hqs	1-12				2 196			
VF Sqs (Army)	1-27				6 1872			
VF (N) Sqdns (Army)	1-67				1 288			
VLR Grp Hqs (Army)	1-112				2 210			
VLR Sqs	1-167				6 3882			
	Total				6448			
A.A. ARTILLERY								
AAA A/W Bn	44-25	1			2 1234			
AAA Gun Bn	44-115				2 1602			
AAA A/W Bn	44-25				1 100			
AAA Btry (- 1 Plat)	44-17				1 65			
Hq & Hq Btry AAA Grp	44-12	801			1 42			
AAA Op Det	44-7							
	Total				3043			From Phase I
ARTILLERY								
155 MM Gun (CA) Bn	4-55	1			1 488			
F.A. Bn (105 MM)	6-25	724			1 482			
	Total				970			From Phase I
ARMORED								
Tank Bn Medium	17-25	1			1 117			From Phase I
Tank Co Medium	17-27				117			From Phase I
AMPH Tk Bn	17-115	1 748						From Phase I
	Total	472			117			

Unit	T/O	ASSAULT			GARRISON			Remarks
		Army	Navy	Marine	Army	Navy	Marine	
AVIATION SERVICE UNITS								
AAF JCC Det	-	1			1 50			
AACS Mobile Unit	1-447s				1 109			
M.P. Co Aviation	19-217				2 202			
Weather Det	-				1 47			
Aviation Sqdn	1-999	50			2 506			
Sta Comp Sqdn	1-497s	1 109			1 103			
Air Serv Grp Hqs	1-452(T)				4 1248			
Air Eng Sq	1-457(T)				4 1032			
Air Mat Sq	1-458(T)				4 568			
Hq & Hq Sq Air Depot Grp	1-852				1 190			
Depot Rep Sq	1-857				1 369			
Depot Sup Sq	1-858				1 131			
Med Sup Plat Avn	8-497				1 21			
QM Trk Co Avn	10-517				2 204			
QM Plat Air Depot Grp	10-427				1 24			
Cml Co Air Op	3-457				1 134			
Sig Co Depot Avn	11-287				1 189			
Det VF Control Sq	1-47				1 25			
Photo Lab Bomb Gp	1-119				2 42			
Total		159			5194			
CHEMICAL								
Chem Bn Motorized	3-25	1 596			1 18			From Phase I
Chem Sup Team Type II	3-500				18			From Phase I
Total		596						
ENGINEER								
Engineer (C) Bn	5-15	3 1911			1 2604			
Hq & Hq Co Eng (C) Grp	5-192	1 81			1 191			
Eng Avn Regt (3 Bns)	5-411				3 321			
Maintenance Co	5-157							
Dump Truck Co	5-88				1 579			
Eng Serv Bn Comp	5-500							

ICEBERG
ANNEX 3 TO APPENDIX H
TROOP LIST - PHASE III - KNOWLEDGE

January 1945

Unit	T/O	ASSAULT Army	ASSAULT Navy	ASSAULT Marine	GARRISON Army	GARRISON Navy	GARRISON Marine	Remarks
ENGINEER (Continued)								
S/L Maint	5-500				1 3			
Eng Const Bn	5-75				2 1800			New units not in assault from Phase I.
NCB	P-1					½ 558		New units not in assault from Phase I.
Eng Avn Bn	5-415	1 777			1 33			From Phase I
Eng Depot Plat	5-47				1 118			From Phase I.
Eng Equip Co L	5-367				1 216			From Phase I
Petrol Dist Co	5-327							From Phase I.
Total		2769			5865	558		Less nurses
MEDICAL								
Evacuation Hosp (Semi)	8-581	1 256			3 984	1 14		Includes 126 nurses to arrive on cell.
G-6(100 beds)Dispensary M.G.	G-6 8-672s							
Port Surg Hosp	3-500	2 74				1 87		
Malaria Control unit	8-500	1 12						
Malaria Survey unit	8-500	1 13	1 87					
G-8 (25 bed) Dispensary M.G.	G-8 8-560							
Sta Hosp (500)								
Mal Control unit	8-500				1 12			
Mal Survey unit	8-500				1 13			
Med Sup Team	8-500	1 23			1 23			
Sanitary Co	8-117				1 112			
Vet Det Food Insp	8-500				1 5			
Surg Team	8-500	3 21			1 157			From Phase I.
Total		399			1149	101		
ORDNANCE								
Heavy Maint Co Tk	9-37	1 202						
Maint Co (AA)	9-217	1 157			1 157			
Ammunition Co	9-17	1 185						
Hq & Hq Det Ord Bn	9-76	1 34			1 34			
Ord MM Co	9-7	1 162			1 162			

Unit	T/O	ASSAULT			GARRISON			Remarks
		Army	Navy	Marine	Army	Navy	Marine	
ORDNANCE								
Hv Auto Maint Co	9-197	-			½			
Ord Ammo (Avn) Co	9-19	-			1			
Ord Depot Co	9-57	1			1			
Bomb Disposal Sq	9-179	2			2			
	Total	14			14			
		180			180			
					179			
					101			
		935			827			
QUARTERMASTER								
QM Trk Co	10-57	2			2			
QM Serv Co	10-67	3			3			
Plat QM Salv Coll Co	10-187	1			1			
QM Dep Sup Co (less 1 Plat)	10-227	1			1			
Plat QM Gr Co	10-297	1			1			
Hq & Hq Det QM Bn	10-536	2			2			
QM Bakery Co	10-147	1			1			
QM Ldy Co	10-167				1			
QM Salv Repr Co(less 1 Plat)	10-237				1			
		220			220			
		636			636			
		56			56			
		142			142			
		23			23			
		60			60			
					168			
					270			
					113			
	Total	1137			1688			
SIGNAL								
JASCO	11-1475	502			1			
Det Sig Serv Co(JCC ≠ S&R)	11-500	150			1			
Signal Constr Co Hvy	11-67	193			1			
Naval Comm Unit						1		
Sig Hvy Const Co Avn	11-67				1			
Det Sig Serv Bn (ΔCS)					1			
Radar Maint Units					3			
	Total	845			678	66		
					250			
					193			
					193			
						66		
					22			
					20			
ADJUTANT GENERAL								
Army Postal Unit Type M	12-605				1			From Phase I.
Base Censorship Det	-				1			
Special Serv Plat	28-17				1			
	Total				74			
					29			
					20			
					25			

Unit	T/O	ASSAULT Army	ASSAULT Navy	ASSAULT Marine	GARRISON Army	GARRISON Navy	GARRISON Marine	Remarks
MILITARY POLICE								
M P Co (Corps)	19-37	1 163			1 344			From Phase I.
M P Bn (less 2 Co) ZI	19-55	1 344						
	Total	507			344			
TRANSPORTATION								
Am Trac Bn	17-125	2 1004						
Port Cos	55-117	2 438			2 438			
Amph Trk Co	55-37	2 360						
Hq & Hq Det Port Bn	55-116	1 33			1 33			
	Total	1835			471			
NAVAL								
CROPAC and attached naval units	-		1 89			704		From Phase I.
Garrison Beach Party	-					1 89		See attached schedule
	Total		89			793		
MILITARY GOVERNMENT								
Interpreters						14		
Mil Govt A Det			1 15			1 15		
Mil Govt B Det			1 27			1 27		
Mil Govt Camp C Det						1 36		
	Total		42			92		
TOTALS		25518	218		30597	1645		
		ASSAULT 25736			GARRISON 32242			
GRAND TOTAL ALL SERVICES								

MIYAKO JIMA

Units	ASSAULT				GARRISON				Differences Assault and Garrison	
	Army	Navy	Marine	Total	Army	Navy	Marine	Total	Decreases	Increases
COMBAT										
Headquarters			1097	1097	542	35		577	1097	577
Divisions, G-2, CIC	14113		34930	49043	14113			14113	34930	
Aviation	4564			4564	10905		340	11245		6681
AA Artillery	1032		4278	5310	5943			5943	4278	4911
Artillery	2192			2192	1249			1249	943	
Armored			1704	1704	724			724	1704	724
Total Combat	21901		42009	63910	33476	35	340	33851	44509	14450
SERVICE										
Aviation	99		294	393	11036		294	11330		10937
Chemical	729			729	403			403	270	
Engineer	2418	2230	1007	5655	17010	2230		19240	1007	15018
Medical	374	261	464	1099	2284	331		2615		1980
Ordnance	2265			2265	1947			1947	887	
Quartermaster	697		2500	3197	3998			3998		369
Signal	1299		1777	3076	925	85		1010	3420	213
Adjutant General					180			180		180
Military Police	798			798	829			829		66
Transportation	3016		2204	5220	1128	274		1402	4125	307
Naval Base Units		178		178	37	2029		2029		1851
Military Gov't		126		126		329		366	84	324
Total Service	11695	2795	8248	22736	39777	5278	294	45349	12322	34935
MIYAKO TOTAL	33596	2795	50255	86646	73253	5313	634	79200	56831	49385

Unit	T/O	ASSAULT Army	Navy	Marine	Army	GARRISON Navy	Marine	Remarks
CORPS HEADQUARTERS (MAR) IS COM HQ	F-850	1		1 1097	1 542	35		From Phase I.
AMPHIBIOUS DIVISIONS (ARMY) 7		1 14032			1 14032			From Area Reserve.
AMPHIBIOUS DIVISIONS (MAR) F-100				2 34930				From Phase I.
G-2 TEAMS		6 31			6 31			
CIC TEAMS		4 50			4 50			
Total		**14113**		**34930**	**14113**			
AVIATION COMBAT UNITS								
Hq & Hq Sq Bomb Wg VLR	1-160-1				1 224			
Hq Bomb Group VLR	1-112				4 420			
Bomb Sq VLR	1-167				12 7764			
Photo Lab Bomb Gp	1-119				4 84			
Hq VF Grp	1-12				2 196			
VF Sq	1-27				6 1872			
VF (N) Sq	1-67				1 288			
Det VF Control Sq	1-47				1 57			
VMB Sq (Mar)	D-103						1 340	
Total					**10905**		**340**	
AA ARTILLERY								
AAA A/W Bn Army	44-25	3 2403			4 3204			
AAA Gun Bn Army	44-115	3 1893			3 1893			
AAA S/L Bn less 1 Btry	44-135				1 578			
Hq & HQ Btry AAA Grp Army	44-12	2 146			2 146			
Opns Det AAA	44-7	1 42			1 42			
AAA HQ & HQ Btry, Brig	44-10-1	1 80			1 80			
Total		**4564**			**5943**			
ARTILLERY								
HQ & HQ Btry Corps Arty	E-149						1 117	From Phase I.
155 MM Gun Bn	E-185						3 2211	From Phase I.
155 MM How Bn	E-135						3 1950	From Phase I.

Unit	T/O	ASSAULT Army	ASSAULT Navy	ASSAULT Marine	GARRISON Army	GARRISON Navy	GARRISON Marine	Remarks
ARTILLERY (Continued)								
8" How Bn (Army)	6-365	1 586			2 1176			2 Bns plus one (1) Batter
Observation Bn (FA)	6-75	1 446			1 73			From Phase I.
155 MM Gun (CA) Bn (Army)	4-55							
HQ & HQ Btry C.A. Gp (Army)	4-62							
Total		1032			1249			
ARMORED								
Tank Bn (Med) (Army)	17-25	1 724						
Amph Tk Bn	17-115	1 748		2 1704	1 724			From Phase I.
Armored Tk Bn	F-1020							
Tank Bn - Armored Flame Thrower	17-25	1 720						
Total		2192		1704	724			
AVIATION SERVICE UNITS								
A.W. Sqdn (Marine)	E-691			294			294	
Signal Co Wing VIR	-(11-247				1 127			
	(11-500							
AACS Mobile Unit	-(11-447s	99			1 135			
Serv Group Hq.	-(1-452-T				6 1872			
Air Material Sq	(1-453-T				6 852			
Air Eng Sq	(1-457-T				6 1548			
Aviation Sqdns	1-999				6 1518			
Chem Co Air Oper	3-457				2 268			
Chem Depot Co Avn	3-418				1 78			
Med Supply Plat Avn	8-497				2 42			
Ord Depot Co Avn	9-57				1 180			
Ord Maint Co Air Force	9-257				1 215			
QM Truck Co Avn	10-517				6 612			
QM Plat Air Depot Gr	10-427				2 48			
Sig Hvy Const Bn (less 1 co)	11-65				1 219			

Unit	T/O	ASSAULT			GARRISON			Remarks
		Army	Navy	Marine	Army	Navy	Marine	
AVIATION SERVICE UNITS (Continued)								
Sig Co Dep Avn	11-287	2			2 378			
MP Co Aviation	19-217	5			5 505			
HQ & HQ Sq Air Depot Grp	1-852	2			2 380			
Depot Rep Sq	1-857	2			2 738			
Depot Sup Sq	1-858	2			2 262			
Sta Complement Sq	1-497s	2			2 206			
Det Weather Sq	1-627	1			1 95			
Cml Maint Co Avn	3-47	1			1 119			
HQ & HQ Co SAW	11-400	1			1 119			
Det Sig Serv Bn ACS	11-500	1			1 22			
Radio Sq Mob (J)	1-1027	1			1 448			
Det Sig Serv Bn JCC	11-500	1			1 50			
Total		99		294	11036		294	
CHEMICAL								
Chemical Bn MTZ (Army)	3-25	1 596			1 130			
Chemical Gen Serv Co	3-137				1 133			
Chemical Smoke Gen Co	3-367	1 133			1 140			
Chem Processing Co	3-77							
Total		729			403			
ENGINEER								
Engineer C Bn	5-15	3 1911			3 1911			
HQ & HQ Co Eng C Grp	5-192	1 81			1 81			
Eng Topo Bn	5-55							
Naval C.B.	F-1	1 426	2 223C			2 2230		
Avn Eng Regt (2 Bns)	5-411				1 6489			From Phase I.
Maint Co	5-157				2 382			
Dump Truck Co	5-88				8 656			
Eng Depot Plat	5-47				1 48			
Eng Const Bn	5-75				6 5400			

Unit	T/O	ASSAULT			GARRISON			Remarks
		Army	Navy	Marine	Army	Navy	Marine	
ENGINEER (Continued)								
Eng Serv Bn Comp	5-500	1 635			1 635			
S/I Maint	5-500	2 6			2 6			
Sep Eng Bn (Corps)	8-235							
Water Sup Co	5-67			1 136	1 136			
HQ & HQ Co Cont Grp	5-72			1 94	1 94			
HQ HQ Co Base Depot	5-592			1 72	1 72			
Co Base Depot	5-267			1 165	1 165			
Co Base Equip	5-377			1 173	1 173			
Co Hevy Shop	5-357			1 171	1 171			
Plat Part Sup	5-567			1 57	1 57			
Co Petrol Dist	5-327			1 216	1 216			
Co Light Equip	5-367			1 118	1 118			
	Total	2418	2230	1007	17010	2230		
MEDICAL								
Corps Evac Hosp	8-510	1 212			1 212			From Phase I.
Field Hospital	G-6		2 261			2 261		Less Nurses.
Dispensary 100 bed M.G.				2 464				1 G-6(100 Beds) ≠ 1 G-6 Aug to 500 beds.
Malaria Control	8-500	1 12			1 12			From Phase I.
Malaria Service	8-500	1 13			1 13			From Phase I.
Sta Hosp (1000)	8-550				1 506			83 nurses to come in later.
Sta Hosp (500)	8-560				4 1144			168 nurses to come in later.
G-7 (50) in Quonset Huts	8-572s					1 70		
Port Surg Hosp	8-117				2 74			
Sanitary Co	8-500				2 224			
Vet Det Food Insp	8-500				1 5			
Med Supply Team #5 (B5)	8-500				1 51			
Med Serv Det 9 teams	8-500	9 63			9 63			
	Total	374	261	464	2284	331		

Unit	T/O	ASSAULT Army		Navy	Marine	GARRISON Army		Navy	Marine	Remarks
ORDNANCE										
Hvy Maint Co (Tk)	9-37	1	202			1	202			
Hvy Auto Maint Co	9-197	2	404			1	202			
Maint Co AA	9-217	1	163			1	163			
Ammunition Co	9-17	2	372			1	186			
Bomb Disposal Sqd	9-179	3	21			3	21			
Hq & Hq Det Ord Gp	9-12	1	51							
Hq & Hq Det Ord Bn	9-76	4	136			2	68			
Ord HM Field Army Co	9-9					1	190			
Ord MM Co	9-7	2	324			2	324			
Ord MM	9-127	2	232			2	232			
Ord Depot Co	9-57	2	360			2	180			
Ord Ammo (Avn) Co	9-17	-	-			1	179			
Total			2265				1947			
QUARTERMASTER										
QM Trk Co (Augmented)	10-57	1	135			4	540			
QM Serv Co	10-67	2	424			8	1696			
Flat QM Salv Coll Co	10-187	1	56							
Det QM Dep Sup Co	10-227	1	40							
Flat QM G.R. Co	10-297	1	23							
Hq & Hq Det QM Bn	10-56	1	19							
Mar Field Depot (Reinf)	E-770				1 2500					
QM Salv Coll Co(less 1 Flat)	10-187					5	95			
QM Dep Sup Co	10-227					1	132			
QM G.R. Co (less 2 Flat)	10-297					1	186			
Hq & Hq Det QM Grp	10-22					1	84			
QM Bakery Co plus 2 Plat	10-147					1	31			
QM Bakery Co plus 2 Plat	10-147					1	250			
QM Ldy Co plus 2 Plat	10-167					1	400			
QM Steril Co	10-177					1	159			
QM Steril Co	10-177					1	96			
QM Steril Co(less 1 Flat)	10-177					1	201			
QM Salv Rep Co	10-237					1	128			
QM Gas Sup Co	10-77									
Total			697		2500		5998			

Unit	T/O	ASSAULT Army	Navy	Marine	GARRISON Army	Navy	Marine	Remarks
SIGNAL								
Corps Sig Bn	E-530	1 502		1 777	1 378			From Phase I.
JASCO	E-518	1 250		2 1000				From Phase I.
Sig Serv Co	11-147s	1 437			1 437			
Sig Const Bn	11-500	1 46			1 46			
Det Sig Repair Co	11-65	1 24			1 24			
Det Sig Depot Co	11-127							
Naval Comm Unit	11-107					1 85		
Radar Maint Unit	11-617	6 40			6 40			
Total		1299		1777	925	85		
ADJUTANT GENERAL								
Army Postal Unit Type K	12-605				3 75			
Base Censorship Det	-				1 80			
Special Service Flat	28-17				1 25			
Total					180			
MILITARY POLICE								
M.P. Battalion less 1 Plat	19-55	1 600			1 600			
M.P. Co Corps	19-37	1 163			1 163			
M.P. Co Special	19-500				1 66			
P.O.W. Proc. Plat.	19-237	1 35						
Total		798			829			
TRANSPORTATION								
Amph Trac Bn (Mar)	E-50							From Phase I.
Amph Trac Bn	17-125	2 1004						
Amph Truck Co (Army)	55-37	5 900			5 1095			
Port Cos	55-117	5 1095		4 2024				3 from Phase I.
Amph Truck Co (Mar)	E-705			1 180	1 33			
Hq & Hq Co Port Bn	55-116							

Unit	T/O	ASSAULT			GARRISON			Remarks
		Army	Navy	Marine	Army	Navy	Marine	
TRANSPORTATION (Continued)								
Hq & Hq Co Amph Truck Bn	55-500	1						
Navy C.B. Spec	F-1	17	¼ 274			274		
Total		3016		2204	1128	274		
NAVAL								
CUB						1448		
Garrison Beach Parties	–		2 178			2 178		
Truck Co (Navy)						1 150		
Base Co (Navy)						1 253		
Total			178			2029		
MILITARY GOVERNMENT								
Mil. Govt A Det			3 45			1 15		
Mil. Govt B Det			3 81			1 27		
Mil. Govt Camp Organ C Det						5 180		
Mil. Govt C Det						1 82		
Mil. Govt D Det						1 25		
Camps, 250 man								
Interpreters	N1A,N5C				37			
Total			126		37	329		
TOTAL		33596	2795	50255	73253	5313	634	
GRAND TOTAL ALL SERVICES		ASSAULT			GARRISON			
		86646			79200			

SUMMARY - ICEBERG TROOP LIST - PHASE IIId

KIKAI SHIMA

Units	ASSAULT				GARRISON				Differences Assault and Garrison	
	Army	Navy	Marine	Total	Army	Navy	Marine	Total	Decreases	Increases
COMBAT										
Headquarters	2072		17465	19537	505	35		540	19537	540
Divisions					8031			8031		8031
Aviation					5112		340	5452		5452
AA Artillery	1491			1491	4591			4591		3100
Artillery					976			976		976
Armored			852	852	570			570	852	570
Chemical Warfare					167			167		167
Total Combat	3563		18317	21880	19952	35	340	20327	20389	18836
SERVICE										
Signal	628		500	1128	860	64		924	500	296
Chemical	129		294	423	130			130	294	130
Aviation			232	232	6766		294	7060		6637
Medical	25	87		112	1235	157		1392		1270
Ordnance					928			928		928
Engineer		1115		1115	8461	1673		10134		10134
Naval Base Units	438		1666	2104		1318		1318		1318
Transportation					1028			1028		1028
Military Police	138		1200	1338	298			298	1200	298
Quartermaster					1953			1953		1953
Adjutant General		42		42	15	139		154		112
Military Government					25			25		25
Total Service	1358	1244	3892	6494	21699	3351	294	25344	4861	23701
KIKAI TOTAL	4921	1244	22209	28374	41651	3386	634	45671	25240	42537

Unit	T/O	ASSAULT Army	ASSAULT Navy	ASSAULT Marine	GARRISON Army	GARRISON Navy	GARRISON Marine	Remarks
ISLAND COMDRS HQ						1 480	1 35	From Phase I.
CIC UNIT	F-100					1 25		
Total						505	35	
AMPHIBIOUS DIVISION				1 17465				
INFANTRY DIV LESS 1 RCT AND 1 BCT	7-11	1 2072			1 8000			
PARACHUTE REGT	7-31							
G-2 TEAMS	-				6 31			
Total		2072		17465	8031			
AVIATION UNITS								
Hq Night Fighter Gp	1-12				1 98			
VFP Group Hq	1-12				4 392			
VF Sqdns	1-37				12 3744			
Hq & Hqs Fighter Wing	1-10-1				1 245			
VF(N) Sqdns (Army)	1-67				2 576			
VMTB Sqdns (Mar)	D-103						1 340	
Fiter Cont Sqdn Det	1-47				1 57			
Total					5112		340	
A.A. ARTILLERY								
Hq & Hq Btry, AAA Brig	44-10-1				1 80			
AAA A/W Bn SM	44-125	1 787			3 2361			
AAA Gun Bn SM	44-115	1 631			2 1262			
AAA S/L Bn less 1 Btry	44-135				1 700			
Hq & Hq Btry AAA Gp	44-12	1 73			2 146			
AAA Opns Det	44-7				1 42			
Total		1491			4591			From Phase I.
ARTILLERY								
155 MM Gun (CA) Bn	4-155				2 976			
Total					976			
ARMORED								
Tank Bn Med (less one Co)	17-25				1 570			

Unit	T/O	ASSAULT Army	ASSAULT Navy	ASSAULT Marine	GARRISON Army	GARRISON Navy	GARRISON Marine	Remarks
ARMORED (Continued)								
Armored Am Trac Bn	F-1020			1 852	570			
Total				852				
AVIATION SERVICE UNITS								
A.W. Sqdn (Marine)	1-447s	1 79	1		1 109			
ACS Mobile Unit		1 50			1 50			
JCC Det, Sig Serv Bn, Avn	1-452-T				5 1560			
Air Serv Group Hq	1-457-T				5 1290			
Air Eng Sqn	1-458-T				5 710			
Air Material Sqdn	1-422				3 309			
Sta. Comp Sqdn	—				1 80			
Weather Det								
Aviation Sqdns	1-999				4 1012			
M.P. Co. Avn	19-217				3 303			
Sig Serv Det, ACS	11-500				1 22			
Hq & Hq Sqdn Air Dep Gp	1-852				1 190			
Dep. Rep. Sqdn	1-853				1 369			
Dep. Sup. Sqdn	1-858				1 131			
Med. Sup. Plat Avn	8-497				1 21			
QM Trk Co Avn	10-517				2 204			
Sig Const Co, Hvy Avn	11-67				1 193			
QM Plat, Air Dep Gp	10-427				1 24			
Sig Depot Co Avn	11-287				1 189			
Total		129			6766		294	
CHEMICAL								
Chem Co Mtzed	3-27				1 167			
Chem Co Gen Serv Serv Unit	3-137				1 130			
Total					297			
ENGINEER								
M.C.B.						1 1115		From Phase I.
Eng Bn 'C'	P-1							
Eng Avn Regt(4 Avn Eng Bns)	5-15	1			2 1274			
Hq & Hq Co Eng C Gp	5-415				1 3381			
Lt Equip Co	5-192				1 81			
	5-367				1 188	1½ 1673		From Phase I.

Unit	T/O	ASSAULT Army	ASSAULT Navy	ASSAULT Marine	GARRISON Army	GARRISON Navy	GARRISON Marine	Remarks
ENGINEER (Continued)								
Eng Const Bn	5-75				2 1800			
Engr Maint Co	5-157				1 191			
Engr Serv Bn Comp	5-88				1 579			
Engr Dump Truck Co	5-500				4 428			
Eng S/L Maint Team	5-47				1 3			
Eng Dep Plat	5-500				1 33			
Parts Supply Plat	5-567				1 57			
Petrol Dist Co	5-327				1 216			
Const Grp Hq & Hq Co	5-72				1 94			
Water Supply Co	5-67				1 136			
Total			1115		8461	1673		
MEDICAL								
Evac Hosp, Corps	8-500				2 74			
Port Surg Hosp	8-500				1 12			
Malaria Control Unit	8-510	1 12			1 13			From Phase I.
Malaria Survey Unit		1 13						From Phase I.
G-6(Aug. to 150 beds)M.G.	G-6			1 232				From Phase I.
Field Hospital (400)			1 87		2 424	1 87		From Phase I.
G-7 (50)	G-7							1 from Phase I.
Sta Hosp (500 bed)	8-560				2 572	1 70		84 nurses to come in later.
Sanitary Co	8-117				1 112			
Vet Det Food Insp					1 5			
Med Supply Team Type 4:	8-500				1 23			From Phase I.
Total		25	87	232	1235	157		
ORDNANCE								
Hvy Maint Co (Tk)	9-37				1 202			
Ordnance MM Co	9-7				1 162			
Hq & Hq Det Ord Bn	9-76				1 34			
Ord Depot Co	9-57				1 180			
Ord Ammo Co	9-17				1 179			
Med Maint Co (AA)	9-217				1 157			

Unit	T/O	ASSAULT Army	ASSAULT Navy	ASSAULT Marine	GARRISON Army	GARRISON Navy	GARRISON Marine	Remarks
ORDNANCE (Continued)								
Bomb Disposal Sqdn	9-500				2 14			From Phase I.
QUARTERMASTER								
Sect QM Trk Co (Augmented)	10-57	1 13						
Plat QM Serv Co	10-67	1 100						
Det QM Dep Sup Co	10-227	1 25						
Mar Field Depot	E-770			1 1200	928			
QM Trk Co (Augmented)	10-57				2 268			
QM Serv Co	10-67				4 876			
Plat QM Salv Coll Co	10-187				1 56			
QM Dep Co Supply	10-227				1 136			
Plat QM G.R. Co	10-297				1 23			
Hq & Hq Det QM En	10-56				2 60			
QM Bakery Co	10-147				1 160			
QM Ldy Co (less 1 Plat)	10-167				1 211			
QM Salv Rep Co (less 1 Plat)	10-237	Total 138		1200	1953			
SIGNAL								
Sig Co Wing	11-247				1 127			
JASCO	B-518			1 500				
Det Sig Serv Co	11-500	1 191			1 266			
Signal Const Bn Hvy	11-65	1 437			1 437			
Naval Comm Unit	11-617					860		From Phase I.
Radar Maint Unit		Total 628		500	4 30	1 64		
ADJUTANT GENERAL								
Army Postal Unit Type K	12-605				Total 1 25	25		
MILITARY POLICE								
MP Co ZI	19-57				Total 2 298	298		

- 160 -

Unit	T/O	ASSAULT Army	ASSAULT Navy	ASSAULT Marine	GARRISON Army	GARRISON Navy	GARRISON Marine	Remarks
TRANSPORTATION								
Hq & Hq Co Amph Trk Bn	55-500				1 17			
Amph Truck Co	55-37				3 540			
Amph Trac Bn	E-50			2 1014				From Phase I.
Amph Trac Co	E-46			2 280				From Phase I.
Amph Truck Co	E-705			2 372				From Phase I.
Port Cos	55-37				2 438			
Hq & Hq Co Port Bn	55-116	2 438			1 33			
Total		438		1666	1028			
NAVAL								
GROPAC						1 459		
PT Operating Bases						2 470		
Boat Pool						1 300		
Garrison Beach Party						1 89		
Total						1318		
MILITARY GOVERNMENT								
Mil Govt A Det			1 15			1 15		
Mil Govt B Det			1 27			1 27		
Mil Govt Camp Orgn C Det						2 72		
Camps 250 man						1 25		
Interpreters	N/A				15			See attached schedule.
Total			42		15	139		
TOTALS		4921	1244	22209	41651	3386	634	
		ASSAULT 28374			GARRISON 45671			
GRAND TOTAL ALL SERVICES								

NAVAL BASE UNIT FOR OKINO DAITO JIMA

GROPAC

		Off.	E.M.	Total
A - 3	Administration (mod.) (1 Officer as Port Director)	4	30	
B - 5A	Boat Pool - including crews for LCM and LCV(P).	2	65	
B - 7	Surface Radar	1	20	
B - 8	Minesweeping	1	1	
D - 10	Storage (mod)	1	8	
D -	Disbursing	1	3	
E - 9	Mobile small boat repair (aug)	1	24	
G - 10	10 Bed dispensary	1	3	
J - 4A	Bomb Disposal	1	1	
J - 4B	Mine Disposal	1	1	
J - 4C	Base Demolition	-	-	
N - 1A	Camp (250 men) modified	-	22	
N - 9	Base Recreation	-	-	
		14	178	192

NAVAL BASE UNITS FOR KUME

GROPAC

		Off.	E.M.	Total
Standard GroPac plus Additional functional components		21	274	
B - 1	HECP	4	23	
B - 3	Underwater Det.	5	24	
J - 12B	Net Component	3	27	
B - 7	Radar (med)	1	20	
B - 8	Minesweeping	1	1	
B - 9	Fleet Moorings	-	-	
B - 10	Nav Aids	-	-	
		35	369	404

Boat Pool (boats supplied by ComPhibsPac)   300

GRAND TOTAL   704

NAVAL BASE UNITS FOR MIYAKO JIMA

CUB

		Off.	E.M.	Total
A - 2	Admin	7	55	
A - 6	Intelligence	2	3	
A - 7	Shore Patrol	3	20	
B - 1	HECP	4	25	
B - 3	Underwater Det.	5	27	
B - 4A	Port Director	10	14	
B - 4C	Harbor Patrol	1	28	
B - 5A	Boat Pool	1	5	
B - 5B	Barge Pool	-	28	
B - 6	Radar	1	46	
B - 8	Minesweeping	1	1	
B - 9	Fleet Moorings	-	--	
B - 10	Navigation Aids	-	--	
D - 2	Supply (modified)	10	75	
D - 4	Tank Farm (modified)	1	11	
D - 15	Cobbler & Tailor Shop	-	5	
D - 22	Disbursing Office	1	5	
E - 8	Small Boat Repair (equip. aug.)	4	64	
E - 9	Small Boat Repair (mot.)	-	18	
E - 16	Oxygen Plant	-	12	
E - 17	Acetylene Plant	-	6	
- 19	Typewriter Repair	-	1	
	Dispensary (100 bed)	8	100	
	First Aid Sub-Dispensary	1	2	
	Sub-Disp. Dental	1	1	
	Gas Tank Farm	-	--	
	Machine Gun	1	5	
	Ammunition Storage	5	10	
	Bomb Disposal	1	1	
	Mine Disposal	1	1	
	Demolition	-	--	
	Mine Assy. Depot (fwd)	3	30	
	Fleet Component	5	45	
	Camp (250 man)	-	25	
	Camp (250 man)	-	--	
	Camp (1000 man)	-	81	
	Camp (1000 man)	-	--	
	Bakery (1000 men)	-	6	
	Base recreation	-	--	
12A	Fire Prot - Basic	1	4	
12C	Fire Prot - Waterfront	-	2	
Q- 2	Pre-embarkation Unit	-	--	
		78	760	848
	Boat Pool (boats supplied by PhibsPac)			600
	GRAND TOTAL			1448

Milton Keynes UK
Ingram Content Group UK Ltd.
UKHW010756080824
446708UK00024B/290

9 781608 883370